# ONE HUNDRED NAMED
# WOMEN
## OF THE
# BIBLE

# ONE HUNDRED NAMED
# WOMEN
## OF THE
# BIBLE

A Stroll through the Bible Highlighting the Lives of Its Women

## Verneva Goss White

**ARPress**

45 Dan Road Suite 5

Canton MA 02021

Hotline:     1(888) 821-0229
Fax:         1(508) 545-7580

Ordering Information:

Quantity sales. Special discounts are available on quantity purchases by corporations, associations, and others. For details, contact the publisher at the address above.

Printed in the United States of America.

ISBN-13:     Paperback     979-8-89356-017-6
             eBook         979-8-89356-018-3

Library of Congress Control Number: 2024902793

# DEDICATION

To my daughters, Naomi Faith White Chancy and Allie Arnell White Copeland, and to all Christian women everywhere.

# ACKNOWLEDGMENT

WRITING THIS BOOK WAS A NEW EXPERIENCE FOR ME.

SINCERE THANKS TO MY HUSBAND, CHARLES WHITE, FOR HIS PATIENCE, ENCOURAGEMENT AND OVERALL SUPPORT DURING MY LONG HOURS OF STUDY AND RESEARCH.

SINCERE THANKS TO THE STAFF AT WESTBOW PUBLISHING FOR THEIR PATIENCE, INSTRUCTION, SUGGESTIONS AND GUIDANCE IN THE WRITING, ARRANGING, DESIGNING AND PRODUCTION OF THIS BOOK.

# INTRODUCTION

*One Hundred Named Women of the Bible* provides insight into the positions held by, influence of, and contributions made by women in biblical times.

Throughout the years, the Bible has been accused of being antifemale. The idea repeated over and over again is that because of the male- dominated culture of the Middle East in biblical times, women were not permitted to have a part in the decision-making process. But upon careful investigation, you will discover that, in spite of cultural circumstances, the Bible is replete with positive experiences of women. Some women mentioned in the Bible had a decidedly profound effect on the events of their time. There were courageous women, bold and daring women, women of influence, virtuous women, and women who were strong in faith and mighty in prayer. They had strengths and weaknesses, were leaders in the right and the wrong, and many times prevailed against insurmountable odds. In many cases, we can see how God overruled events and circumstances to magnify His own glory in the outcome of biblical women's lives.

The purpose of this book is not just to present information but also to educate, inspire, and impart life lessons. This is not a book that promotes bias. It reveals the good, the bad, and the indifferent.

I have chosen a hundred notable women to talk about. There are many others mentioned in the Bible, although not every book of the Bible contains women.

I hope that you will gain a new perspective on the gifts, capabilities, and responsibilities that God gave women in Bible times. God gives women today the same things, if not more, because of our culture and exposure. "To whom much is given, much is expected" (Luke 12:48).

The hundred women I discuss are not presented in alphabetical order; rather, they are listed in order of the book of the Bible in which their names appear. In some instances, there is more than one woman bearing the same name. In these cases, I identify which woman is being spoken of by including clarifying information in the chapter title.

My hope is that readers of this book will gain a greater appreciation of the contributions made by our female ancestors and also be inspired to move forward in fulfilling their individual, God-designed destinies.

My life was greatly enriched in doing the research to write this book. I pray that your life will be greatly enriched by reading it.

Now let's take a stroll through the Bible, highlighting the lives and experiences of these hundred named women.

Happy reading!

# CONTENTS

# R

# Women in the Old Testament

The Bible consists of sixty-six books, thirty-nine in the Old Testament and twenty-seven in the New Testament. Out of the thirty-nine books in the Old Testament, two are named in honor of illustrious women, Ruth and Esther. It speaks volumes of Ruth's and Esther's intelligence and character that their books were included in the Bible even though they lived in a male-dominated society.

Ruth was a Moabite who married a Jewish man who passed away at an early age. Because of her commitment to and support of her aged mother-in-law, and through the providence of God, Ruth became a fore parent of our Lord and Savior, Jesus Christ, by marrying Boaz, the grandson of Rahab and the grandfather of King David.

Esther, through a series of circumstances orchestrated by God, became the reigning queen of Persia, the leading world empire, shortly after the time of the Jewish exile in Babylon when a large number of Jews were still occupying Persia.

# EVE

*Genesis 1–4*

Eve is the mother of all human beings, living and dead. Being the first woman, Eve had no genetic sin. Coming from the hand of God, Eve had an advantage no other woman has ever had. She was pure and holy, with her reflection of the Divine unimpaired. She was the crowning achievement of God's creation. Although created sinless, Eve became the world's first sinner. She introduced sin to her husband and her offspring, and thus all human beings who came after Eve were "shapen in iniquity and conceived in sin" (Psalm 51:5).

"So God created man in his own image, in the image of God created He him; male and female created He them" (Genesis 1:27). "And Adam called his wife's name " Eve" because she was the mother of all living" (Genesis 3:21). Eve was created not as a baby, not as a child, but as a full-grown adult—a woman and wife. She was perfect in body and mind. And it is from her story that we gain insight into life, temptation, sin, and death.

When God placed Adam in the beautiful garden He had created, He gave Adam permission to eat freely of every tree in the garden except for the Tree of the Knowledge of Good and Evil. God gave this instruction to Adam before Eve was created. Evidently, Adam passed this information on to Eve, because she quotes it to the serpent in Genesis 3:2–3.

Scripture is silent about the length of time that Adam and Eve were in the garden before sin crept in. It is said that woman is alert to attractiveness and beauty to a much greater degree than man. Satan knew this. So he approached Eve instead of her husband, Adam. He reasoned that only through Eve would he be able to seduce Adam.

Looking at the tree, Eve thought that it was pleasant to the eyes. Satan, observing her, said, "It is good for food. Eating from it will make one wise." The tree appealed to Eve's eyes and captured her curiosity. She saw, she desired, and then she took.... Once she ate the fruit from the tree, lust was indulged and sin was conceived. But Eve didn't stop at eating the fruit herself, she gave it to Adam, and he ate of it, also. Adam was not deceived by Satan, but Eve was. Eve had made the mistake of wandering onto forbidden ground and parlaying with the serpent and got caught up in his lies causing her to be deceived.. On the other hand, when Eve brought the fruit to Adam and related her story, Adam immediately recognized that the serpent was Satan, but because of his love for Eve and his weakness of faith in God to supply his human needs, he yielded to the temptation and did eat.

Because of Adam and Eve's sin, their happiness didn't last long. Fear, guilt, and shame caused them to hide themselves from the once welcome and anticipated presence of God. **Sin always separates people from God**. Adam blamed Eve and God for his actions. Adam said to God, "This woman you gave me to be with me, she gave me of the tree and I did eat" (Genesis 3:12). Eve blamed the serpent. The once happy couple were driven from their beautiful garden home to a world of thorns and thistles. Paradise was lost to Adam and Eve because they disobeyed God.

But in deep compassion and tender mercy, God looked down upon our fore parents and declared a glorious promise: To satan He said, "And I will put enmity between you and the woman, and between your seed and her Seed; He shall bruise your head and you shall bruise His heel.(Gen. 3:15)" To Satan, this was God's judgment call; to Adam and Eve, it was hope.

When Cain was born, Eve exclaimed, "I have gotten a man from the Lord," thinking that this child was the promised seed. How deep her grief and disappointment must have been many years later when her firstborn murdered his brother and became a fugitive.

Adam and Eve lived for hundreds of years. They no doubt had other children. When Adam was 130 years old, Eve gave birth to Seth. Joyfully, Eve exclaimed, "God has given me another seed instead of Abel, whom Cain slew." **Through the lineage of Seth was born the Seed, Jesus the Christ.**

Eve's name is mentioned in the New Testament, in 2 Corinthians 11:3, as a warning to Christians that they not be led away from spiritual paths by the subtlety of modern-day serpents.

Despite Eve's transgressions, she stands as an example of our Father's grace and mercy in empowering all human beings to rise above sin. **"If we confess our sins, He is faithful and just to forgive us our sins and to cleanse us from all unrighteousness" (1 John 1:9).**

The author, here, will expound upon two very special gifts that God gave to Adam and Eve in the garden, and after the fall, they brought with them outside the gates of paradise, and these gifts still remain with us today: **Marriage** and the **Sabbath**.

**Marriage.** After Adam was created, he was given the privilege and responsibility of naming all the animals. As they passed before him, he noticed that each one had been given a companion, but there was not found any companion for him, for there was none equal to him. There was no one of the same nature to love and to be loved. God said, "It is not good that man should be alone, so He made Adam a companion. Someone like him, yet opposite him that would compliment him in fulfilling the command be fruitful and multiply. In other words, a male and a female, the only type of marriage that can pro-create – not two men or two women. Eve was created with a rib taken from the side of Adam, indicating that she was not to control him as the head, nor to be trampled under his feet as an inferior, but to stand by his side as an equal. God created and celebrated the first marriage. God the creator of the universe is it's originator. Marriage is honorable. Therefore shall a man leave his father and his mother and shall cleave unto his wife; and they shall be one. When these divine principles are recognized and obeyed in the marriage relation, marriage will be a blessing; it will guard the integrity and well being of the race, it will provide for man's social needs and elevate the physical, intellectual and moral nature. It can be a little heaven on earth.

**Sabbath.** After the creation was complete, God saw everything that He had made, and behold, it was very good. In six days the great work of creation had been accomplished. Then God rested on the seventh day from all His work which He had made. And God blessed the seventh day and sanctified it because that in it He had rested from all His work which God created and made. He rested not as one tired or weary, but as one well pleased with the fruits if His wisdom and goodness and the manifestations of His glory. Following the example of the Creator, man is to rest upon this sacred day, that as he should look upon the heavens and the earth, he might reflect upon God's work of creation; and that as he should behold the evidences of God's wisdom and goodness, his heart might be filled with love and reverence for his maker. In placing His blessing upon the seventh day, God set up a memorial of His work of creation and redemption. God's blessings and sanctification(holiness) cannot be transferred to any other day. God knew that the Sabbath was essential for man, even in Paradise. Man needed to lay aside his own interests and pursuits for this one day , that he might more fully contemplate the works of God and meditate upon His power and goodness. Man needed the Sabbath to remind him more deeply of God and to awaken gratitude within him because all that he enjoyed and possessed came from the beneficent and merciful hand of the Creator.

# ADA AND ZILLAH (AND NAAMAH)

*Genesis 4:19–24*

Ada and Zillah were Lamech's (seventh generation from Adam) two wives. (This Lamech was Cain's off spring). Theirs was the first polygamous marriage recorded in the Bible. This union was in direct disobedience to God's commands. It degraded the dignity of womanhood and also destroyed true family values by injecting immorality into future generations.

Ada gave birth to two sons, Jabal and Jubal. Scripture does not say whether or not they were twins. Jabal raised livestock and lived in tents. Jubal was a musician who played the harp and flute.

Zillah bore two children also, a boy and a girl. Tubal-Cain, her son, was an instructor of every craftsman in bronze and iron. His sister's name was Naamah. Nothing is mentioned in Scripture about Naamah's gifts and qualities, but we can be sure that she had some, since her brothers were talented.

Tubal's name is a hyphenate including "Cain" in order to perpetuate Tubal's infamous forefather's name, lest future generations forget.

Lamech wrote the following poem to his wives:

> Ada and Zillah, listen to me;
> Wives of Lamech, listen to my speech!
> For I have killed a man for wounding me,
> Even a young man for hurting me.
> If Cain shall be avenged sevenfold,
> Seventy-seven fold if anyone kills me.

God had said earlier that a person who killed Cain would be punished sevenfold. Lamech's saying that a person would be punished seventy-sevenfold for killing him seems to indicate that he thought his life was worth ten times more than Cain's.

This poem is full of pride and arrogance. It is indicative of the kind of character Lamech possessed, one that was temperamental and vindictive. The bottom line is that Lamech was a killer. Like grandfather, like grandson!

This real-life illustration is indicative of the types of people who lived on earth just before the flood. Lamech is the last person mentioned in Cain's genealogy. This was when the sons of God (Seth's line) saw that the daughters of men (Cain's line) were fair, so they took wives of their own choosing (Genesis 6:2, 7:7). "And God said I will destroy man whom I have created from the face of the earth."

Be careful in choosing a spouse/life partner. Your choice has a significant bearing on the spiritual and physical quality as well as the quantity of your life. It could be long and bountiful, short and grievous or somewhere in between.

# SARAH

*Genesis 11:29–31; 12:5–17; 16:1–8; 18:6–15; 20:2–18;21:1–12;23:1, 2, 9; 25:10–12*
*1 Peter 3:6*

Sarah, the mother of nations, was Abraham's wife and also his sister. The two had the same father, Terah, but not the same mother. Their mothers' names are not mentioned in Scripture.

Almost every experience of Abraham was an experience of Sarah, as well. She shared his agonies and his ecstasies and also shared in the covenant promise: she would be the mother of nations.

The couple's story begins when Abraham is seventy-five years of age and Sarah is sixty-five years old. The Lord had said to Abram:

> Get out of your country, from your family and from your father's house, to a land that I will show you. I will make you a great nation, I will bless you and make your name great, and you shall be a blessing. I will bless those who bless you and I will curse him who curses you and in you all the families of the earth shall be blessed. Gen. 12:1-3.

So Abram departed as the Lord had told him to. He took Sarah, his wife, with him.

Abraham is the first man in Scripture to be referred to as a Hebrew. As his wife, Sarah is the first Hebrewess. Together, they were the co- founders of the great Hebrew nation.

Even at the age of sixty-five, Sarah possessed a physical beauty so remarkable that Abraham feared that other powerful men would desire her for themselves. He was right. When Sarah accompanied Abraham to Egypt, he passed her off as his sister because he feared the Egyptians would kill him if they knew she was his wife. Years later, he did the same thing at the court of Abimelech, King of Gerar. In each situation, dreadful wrong was averted only by God's intervention. Taking into consideration the biblical account, it is clear that Sarah was an extraordinarily beautiful woman who seemed to grow more attractive with passing years.

The couple's names were originally Abram and Sarai. God changed their names, giving them sacramental names, so-called because they were inspired and associated with a particular promise, covenant, or declaration of God as to the character, destiny, or mission of those distinctly named. Abram's name was changed to Abraham, meaning "father of nations." Sarai's name was changed to Sarah, meaning "a princess—the source of nations and kings."

The one great anxiety of Abraham and Sarah was that they had had no children throughout their long life together, even though God had promised that Abraham would be the father of a great nation and that his seeds would be as the sand of the sea. Sarah was barren. To a Hebrew woman in biblical times, barrenness was regarded as a sign of God's disfavor.

Sarah felt that she had a key role to play in God's plan for Abraham, because Abraham could never become the patriarch of a great nation if she could not become mother to his offspring. So she persuaded Abraham to take her handmaid, Hagar, as a concubine. He did. According to the laws of that time, a son born of Hagar in this circumstance was regarded as the son and heir of Abraham and Sarah. As you can see, surrogate mothers are not a new idea.

After Hagar conceived, she treated her mistress with such contempt that Sarah drove her from the house. Hagar, however, returned at God's command, submitted herself to Sarah, and gave birth to Ishmael.

Afterward, when Sarai was about ninety, God promised her a son; her name was changed to Sarah. A year later, Isaac, the child of promise, was born.

Although Sarah gave birth to only one son (Isaac), she did become the mother of nations. Isaac had two sons: Jacob and Esau. Jacob had twelve sons who each became the leader of one of twelve tribes. In the seventh chapter of Revelation, the names of those tribes/sons are listed over the entrance to the heavenly city—on the twelve gates. It is through Jacob that we trace the lineage of Jesus Christ.

Sarah had her faults true enough. Her faith, at times, grew weak. Her own heart sometimes led both her and her husband astray. Fortunately, there was much more to Sarah than her faults. She had strengths as well as weaknesses. Scripture commends her for her faith and steadfastness. The apostle Peter points to her as a model of how every wife should submit to her husband's leadership. Sarah's life on the whole is characterized by humility, loyalty, faithfulness, deep affection for her husband, sincere love for God, and a hope that would not die.

Sarah died at the age of 127. She was buried at Machpelah. Abraham had purchased the cave of Machpelah, near the oak of Mamre, as a family burial ground. Sarah is the only woman in the Bible whose age at the time of her death is recorded.

Only two women are honored to have their names listed by the writer in the book of Hebrews' " hall of faith "- Sarah's is the first; Rahab's, the second (Hebrews 11:11, 31).

# HAGAR

*Genesis 12:10–20; 14:4; 16:1–26; 21:1–21*

Hagar was Sarah's Egyptian maid.

God had promised to Abraham a son who would be his heir, but Sarah was barren. So following the marital customs of that time, Sarah gave Hagar to her husband as a secondary wife. Remember, such an action was not supposed to be the custom of God's people. But usually when a person response to the call of God on one's life, one sometimes brings a lot of baggage along. At the time when Hagar realized she was pregnant with Ishmael, she despised her mistress. This caused trouble. Hagar was driven out, but an angel of the Lord appeared to her and sent her back to her mistress, Sarah, telling her to humble herself. And she obeyed.

When Ishmael was fourteen years old, Abraham was one hundred and Sarah was ninety. This was when Isaac was born. When Isaac became of age to be weaned, the custom was that a feast be given in his honor. Ishmael belittled the event. Sarah insisted that he be sent away. With a heavy heart, Abraham reluctantly complied with his wife's wishes and sent Hagar and Ishmael away.

Remember, God does not need any help carrying out His plans. We only get in His way and complicate things, and then He has to clean up the results of our indiscretions, just as He did with Abraham and Sarah.

Isaac's wife, Rebekah, gave birth to Jacob and Esau (twins). Jacob gave Isaac twelve grandsons who became leaders of twelve tribes. It is through Jacob and not Esau, that we trace the lineage of Jesus Christ.

God promised Abraham that Ishmael, though not the child of promise, would also become the father of a great nation. "Twelve princes shall he beget" (Genesis 17:20). The names of these princes were Nebajoth, Kedar, Adbeel, Mibsam, Mishma, Dumah, Massa, Hadar, Tema, Jetur, Naphish, and Kedemah (Genesis 25:13–16)— twelve princes of twelve respective nations.

In Galatians 4:21–5:1, Paul uses the story of Hagar and Sarah as an illustration of the law, comparing a child of flesh (Ishmael) to a grace-child of the Spirit (Isaac).

# MILCAH

*genesis 11:27–29; 22:20–30*

Milcah was Abraham's niece, the daughter of his brother Haram, who died. She was also the sister of Lot. She married her uncle Nabor, Abraham's brother, and bore him eight sons: Huz, Buz, Kemuel, Chesed, Hazo, Pildash, Jidlaph, and Bethuel. Bethuel begot Rebekah and Laban. So Milcah was the great-grandmother of Jacob, Rachel, and Leah, which means, they were cousins.

Please note that Rebekah and Laban both practiced deception. Rebekah showed favoritism for her son Jacob and devised a scheme to deceive Isaac, his father, into giving Jacob the birthright/blessing that was due Esau as the elder son. Laban deceived Jacob, after the latter labored seven years for the former, into marrying Leah, his oldest daughter, instead of Rachel, the one they had agreed on and the one Jacob loved.

Could the deception practiced by Rebekah and Laban have possibly been a result of the training they received in the home—by precept and example? Parents, beware of not only what you verbally teach your children, but also of what they see you do.

# REBEKAH

*Genesis 22:23; 24:15–67; 26:7–11, 35; 27:5–17, 29, 42–46; 28:2, 3, 5*

Rebekah was the daughter of Bethuel, who was the son of Abraham's brother Nabor and his wife, Milcah. The sister of Laban, Rebekah became the wife of Isaac and the mother of twin sons, Esau and Jacob.

When Sarah was 127 years old, she died. Abraham and Isaac were probably very lonely after her death. Isaac was now in his manhood. Isaac was the child of promise for whom his father wanted a good wife. In biblical times in the Middle East, parents usually chose wives for their sons as well as husbands for their daughters.

The women who lived in Canaan were idol worshipers. As such, they could not teach their children to love and worship the true God. As Christians, we see in this story how difficult it is for a man or woman to have absolute integrity in his or her faith when he or she does not have a spouse of like faith.

Eliezer, Abraham's trusted servant of many years, was asked to journey back to Haran and try to find a God-fearing wife for Isaac. God had made a great promise to Abraham. He had clearly made known that it was through Isaac, not Ishmael, that the promise would be fulfilled. So Abraham worked with God, not against Him, to bring this about.

The faithful servant, Eliezer made the long journey to Haran. He asked God to direct him to a girl who was generous and kind and willing to serve. Eliezer had a great interest in the situation, too. He had been a servant in Abraham's household since the time before Isaac was born. At Haran, no sooner had Eliezer finished praying than a beautiful young girl with a pitcher on her shoulder came to the well. Her name was Rebekah. Eliezer was both a stranger to her and an old man. This was the test, and Rebekah did not fail. She spoke kindly to Eliezer and offered to draw water for his camel. When Eliezer discovered that Rebekah was the granddaughter of Nabor, Abraham's brother, he knew that his prayer had been answered.

Rebekah invited Eliezer to her home. Once they arrived, Rebekah's parents offered Eliezer food. But he could not eat. He first had to tell them about his mission, with all of the details. Rebekah's parents, too, felt that the hand of the Lord was with them. They left the decision to go or not to go to Rebekah. After all, she was a strong-minded and decisive young woman. Her answer was, "I will go." And she did. At the appointed time, the family said good-bye to Rebekah and sent her away with her attending maid, Deborah.

When Eliezer, Rebekah, and Deborah came near to the home of Abraham and Isaac, it was late afternoon. Isaac was meditating alone in the fields. When he saw the camels coming, he hurried out to meet the small group. Rebekah dismounted her camel and, no doubt, covered her face with her veil, as the custom was. Isaac took her to his mother's tent. Shortly thereafter, Rebekah became his wife, one whom he loved. In this, Isaac was comforted after his mother's death (Genesis 24:67).

After twenty long years, finally a change took place in Rebekah's and Isaac's home. At last, Rebekah became a mother. She gave birth to twins, Esau and Jacob. Usually, children are the link that brings parents closer together, but this was not the case for

Isaac and Rebekah. They were pushed apart, not because of the boys, but because each parent picked a favorite. What an ungodly mistake.

Esau, the older son, was Isaac's favorite. Jacob, the younger, was Rebekah's favorite. Rebekah observed the difference in her two sons. Esau's disposition was secular, while Jacob's disposition was contemplative. She realized that Esau lived only for today, while Jacob had goals for the future. Also, Esau chose two wives who were Canaanite women. Rebekah remembered that the Lord had said to her, "The elder shall serve the younger." Rebekah, perhaps, thought that Esau was not worthy of the blessing of the birthright.

The birthright consisted of receiving a double portion of the inheritance and becoming the spiritual leader (patriarch) of the family upon the death of the father.

One day, Rebekah heard Isaac say to Esau, who was an excellent cook, "bring me venison, and make me savory meat, that I may eat and bless thee before I die." These words pierced Rebekah's innermost being. After hearing them, she forced herself to think fast. She began to plot and scheme to obtain the birthright for her favorite son. She remembered Isaac's failing eyesight. *I will cook meat and season it to smell and taste like Esau's meat and I will dress Jacob in Esau's clothes that bear Esau's smell,* Rebekah thought. Jacob, when confronted with his mother's proposition, was afraid to try to deceive Jacob, his father. He thought he might be discovered and receive a curse instead of a blessing. But his mother insisted. She said, "Upon me be thy curse." Isaac was suspicious of the scheme, but Jacob obeyed his mother. The scheme was a success, if you want to call it that.

After this time, Esau's heart was filled with hatred for his brother. He thought to kill Jacob after his father died. Then he would have all the possessions that rightly belonged to him. With these thoughts in his head, he was consoled. For fear that Esau would harm Jacob, his mother sent him away to his uncle Laban for a little while—or so she thought—until Esau's anger receded.

"Go away for a few days till Esau forgets," Rebekah said. Jacob said good-bye to his parents and started on his long journey, about five hundred miles, thinking that he would return in a few days. The days became weeks, the weeks became months, and the months became years—twenty years, to be exact. Rebekah never saw her beloved favorite son, Jacob, again. She died before he returned. What a tragedy! The whole situation had gotten out of control. The curse was not only on Rebekah's head, but also upon the heads of Jacob, Esau, and Isaac. Theirs became a bitterly divided family forever. Rebekah's motives were selfish; she had been seeking a high spiritual destiny for her favorite son. Instead of yielding the situation to God and waiting upon the Lord for the fulfillment of His promise, however, she thought to assist God in keeping His promise. That's a no-no!

Some people may attempt to justify Rebekah's actions by saying that she chose the course she did because of the prediction God had made: "The elder shall serve the younger." But God has no need of trickery or deceit to fulfill His promises. He is God all by Himself. He doesn't need anybody else! Rebekah sacrificed the love of her husband, the respect of her elder son, and the peace of her soul for the idolized son whose face she never saw again. The strong- minded, decisive girl had grown into a manipulating matriarch and, no doubt, ended her days a brokenhearted woman.

This story is a lesson to all parents to show no favoritism in the family. It could lead to vengeance and remorse in later life. All children should be precious to their parents. If there is partiality shown to any member of a family, it should be only for those who have some type of disability.

# DEBORAH

*Genesis 24:59; 35:8*

In wealthy Hebrew or Jewish homes in biblical times, there was usually a maid. Also, when a daughter was betrothed in marriage, it was customary for the maid to go with the bride to her new home. This was the case for Deborah.

As Rebekah's nurse, Deborah accompanied her mistress to her new home to marry Isaac. When Jacob and Esau were born, Deborah was there to assist. She saw the favoritism that was practiced in this home between the two parents and their two sons, and from time to time, she perhaps gave some subtle counsel that went unheeded. It grieved her deeply to see Jacob having to flee, in fear for his life because of his avenging brother, Esau. When Deborah was old, she was not pushed aside but was considered as a member of the family. The fact that she remained a member of Jacob's household until she died could possibly be because Isaac and Rebekah were both deceased.

According to some writers, Deborah was mourned for as one of the family. Great honor was paid to her at her death. Her name and the place of her burial are recorded in the words of the Scripture that states, "Deborah, Rebekah's nurse, died, and she was buried beneath Bethel under an oak tree whose name Jacob called Allon-bachuth, which means 'oak of weeping.'"

Deborah may be the only maid whose death and burial are recorded in Scripture, which is indicative of how highly esteemed she was by the family she served.

The God of heaven enabled Deborah to live a long life as a devoted, quiet, and faithful maid servant . Through her faith and integrity in God, she transformed herself from someone bonded in servitude to a much appreciated and respected member of the family. Deborah was forever attached to the family by bonds of love and gratitude.

Deborah seems to have taken advice that Paul wrote some thousand years later: "And whatever you do, do it heartily, as to the Lord and not to men, Knowing that from the Lord you will receive the reward of the inheritance; for you serve the Lord Christ" (Colossians 3:23–24).

# KETURA

*Genesis 25:1–6*
*1 Chronicles 1:32–33*

When Abraham was 137 years of age and Sarah was 127, Sarah died and was buried in Machpelah. Abraham married again. His second wife's name was Ketura. Since Ketura was of childbearing age, she was evidently quite a few years younger than Abraham. To this couple were born six sons, whose names were Zimran, Jokshan, Medan, Midian, Ishbak, and Shuah. These six sons became the progenitors of six Arabian tribes of southern and eastern Palestine. The Midianites in Bible times were one of the six tribes.

What an honor it must have been for Ketura to marry someone of great influence and status, a man who had walked and talked with God, a man by whom all nations of the earth would be blessed. Then again, it must have been a little disappointing to Ketura that neither of her sons had a share in God's promise.

The *Seventh-Day Adventist Commentary* states,

> Toward the close of Abraham's life he appointed Isaac, his legal heir and bequeathed to him most of his property. To the sons of Hagar and Keturah he gave token gifts. Presumably, each son received sufficient for a good start in life.

Sending these other sons eastward, while he lived was a precaution against strife after his death, particularly in respect to the right of Isaac, the son of promise, to the land of Canaan.

Abraham was not only the father of faith; he was also a man of great wisdom. He set a good example for parents with two or more children, and especially stepchildren of blended families, as he made a will so that there would be no confusion or disagreements after his death.

The Bible gives no background information on Ketura. And after Abraham's death, nothing else is revealed about Ketura. She dropped in and then dropped out of the story. She fulfilled her role as wife, mother, and perhaps nursemaid of her elderly husband and patriarch, Abraham, the father of the faithful.

# Esau's Three Wives;
## Ada, Aholibamah, and Bashemath

*Genesis 26:34; 36:2-25*

Esau was the first born of twin sons born to Isaac and Rebekah. His brother was Jacob. In Middle Eastern culture in biblical times, it was the norm for parents to become involved in choosing spouses for their daughters as well as their sons. Such was the case with Jacob, the younger brother of Esau. But not so with Esau. He chose his own wife, as he was his own man.

Jacob married within the family and within the faith. Esau regarded not the wishes or wisdom of his parents, as he married whom he chose. I suppose his bitter experience with Jacob and his mother, Rebekah, had some bearing on his actions. He was somewhat of a wild man who never repented of his wrongdoings. He never permitted God to be the Lord of his life. Although Jacob's natural character was worse than Esau's, Jacob saw his own bad actions and repented. God said in Romans 9:13, "I have loved Jacob and hate Esau." What? God hated someone? The correct interpretation of this is, of course, that God loved Jacob's ways—after he repented, of course—and hated Esau's ways because he never repented or gave his heart to God.

Esau became the father of the Edomite nation, and Jacob became the progenitor of the Hebrew, or Israelite, nation. These are Esau's wives:

1. Ada, daughter of Elon the Hittite and mother of Eliphaz

2. Aholibamah, daughter of Anah, the daughter of Zibeon the Hivite; Aholibamah was the mother of Jeush, Jaalan, and Korah

3. Bashemath, Ishmael's daughter and the mother of Reuel

In some cultures, a woman's entire name was changed when she married, which may account for the fact that each of Esau's wives has a name in the genealogy that is different from her name in the historical record.

# RACHEL AND LEAH

*Genesis 29:6–32; 30:1–25; 31:4–32; 35:16–26*

Rachel and Leah were sisters and were the daughters of Laban, the brother of Rebekah. Thus, Rachel and Leah were first cousins of Jacob. Leah possessed great internal beauty. Rachel's outward appearance was extremely beautiful.

The story begins when Jacob has to leave home suddenly to flee from the wrath of his brother Esau, because of trickery. Jacob and his mother, Rebekah, had stolen Esau's birthright. Rebekah sent Jacob to Laban, her brother who lived at Haram, so he could stay there, supposedly for a little while, until everything cooled down. But as the story goes, he was there for twenty years.

When Jacob arrived, the first family member he met was Rachel. Because of her beauty, he evidently fell in love with her that day. He bargained with Uncle Laban to let him work for seven years without pay. Part of the agreement was that at the end of the seven years, Jacob would receive Rachel as his wife. O what a happy day that would be. Herbert Lockyer provides a little background and discusses what happened next: "In that culture, the bride is completely covered. It was the custom of the times for the bride to enter the bedchamber of her husband in silence and darkness. It was only with the morning light that Jacob discovered that he had been deceived by Laban when he saw not Rachel but Leah."

Laban justified his deceptive act by telling Jacob that the younger girl (Rachel) could not be given in marriage before the firstborn (Leah). It was the custom. But, somehow, Laban conveniently had forgotten to tell Jacob about this. Poor, love-starved Jacob accepted his uncle's explanation and agreed to work another seven years without pay in order to marry Rachel. We are not told if Leah or Rachel was in on this deception or not. The two might have been just pawns in the game. It is also worth noting that perhaps this deception brought to Jacob's mind how he had deceived his father, Isaac, years earlier. Maybe he attributed his delay in marrying Rachel to a retributive act of God.

After another seven years, Rachel became Jacob's bride. Then the trouble began. Because of her beauty, Rachel was shown favoritism by Jacob, although Leah held the position of first wife. Leah gave birth to four sons, Reuben, Simeon, Levi, and Judah, hoping to prove herself superior to her sister. After it appeared that she could not have any more children, she gave her handmaid, Zilpah, to Jacob as a secondary wife. Zilpah had two sons with Jacob for Leah: Gad and Asher.

Rachel had no children at this time. To a Hebrew woman in biblical times, this was considered a shame, as she would be looked upon as not serving her purpose in life. Rachel envied her sister. She said to Jacob, "Give me children or I die" (Genesis 30:1)! Jacob was perturbed by her statement. He answered, "Am I in God's stead, who has withheld from thee the fruit of the womb?" So Rachel gave her maid, Bilhah, to Jacob as a secondary wife. Bilhah bore Jacob two sons, Dan and Naphtali.

Polygamy was widespread in the land at that time. It was generally accepted by people, but not by God.

After these two incidents, Leah gave birth to two more sons, Isaacar and Zebelon, and one daughter, Dinah, for a total of eight sons and one daughter. And, at last, Rachel gave birth to Joseph and then Benjamin. She died giving birth to the latter. This is the first recorded incident of a woman's dying in childbirth. As Rachel was dying, she named her baby Benoini, meaning "child of grief." The baby's father, Jacob, changed the name to Benjamin, meaning "child of joy."

Leah, though physically unattractive and perhaps repulsive to others, possessed a deep, abiding inner beauty that Rachel lacked.

Rachel gave birth to Joseph, a deliverer of Israel, a type of Christ. Leah gave birth to Judah, through whose lineage God's promise was fulfilled and the Savior of the world was born.

# BILHAH AND ZILPAH

*Genesis 29:24-29; 30:3-10; 35:22, 25, 26; 37:2; 46:18, 25*

Bilhah and Zilpah were two women in the shadows - the shadows of Rachel and Leah, two bickering, competitive sisters.

Bilhah was a maid from Laban's house who was given to Rachel as a handmaid when the latter became the wife of Jacob. Likewise, Zilpah was given to Rachel's sister Leah as a handmaid.

These two women, Rachel and Leah, were caught up in a big dispute while engaged in a competition of having babies. Being able to have children was considered a sign of approval from God and men alike. But having children was something that the beautiful Rachel could not do.

After Leah had four sons and it seemed that she would not have another, she, like Sarah, encouraged her husband to take Zilpah as a secondary wife. Zilpah gave birth to two sons, Gad and Asher. After this, Leah gave birth to three more children, two sons and a daughter. She named her daughter Dinah.

Rachel was barren for many years. She, too, offered her maid, Bilhah, as a second wife for Jacob. Bilhah conceived and gave birth to two sons, Dan and Naphtali. Rachel later gave birth to Joseph and Benjamin. It was with Bilhah, after the death of Rachel, that Reuben defiled his father's bed, which caused him to lose his birthright (Genesis 35:22).

It must have been an awful existence for Bilhah and Zilpah to live in such a contentious and dysfunctional household where they had very little say about anything, not even their own bodies. I imagine that theirs was a debasing servitude.

Because Leah and Rachel were the primary wives, they were credited with being the mothers of the twelve tribes. Biblical records bear witness to the fact that Bilhah and Zilpah gave birth to four of the twelve sons of Jacob. Even though they did not receive recognition for their efforts, their contributions are defined by the accomplishments of their offspring. Listed below are the names of those four tribes, followed by the names of notable personalities therefrom:

- Gad – Bani, a member of King David's special fighting force of thirty mighty men. This was a great honor and a much coveted position (2 Samuel 23:36).

- Asher – Anna the prophetess (Luke 2:36)

- Dan – Samson the judge (Judges 13:1, 2, 24, 25)

- Naphtali – Barak, the military commander under Deborah (Judges 4:6)

Bilhah's and Zilpah's names are memorialized by the legacy of their offspring.

# DINAH

*Genesis 30:21; 34:1-31*

Dinah was the only daughter of Jacob and Leah. She had twelve brothers. Her love for excitement caused a series of unfortunate events. Her curiosity about her new hometown of Sechem caused her to leave her parents' tent without permission to investigate the nearby town of Sechem. Sechem was an Edomite town founded by the offsprings of Esau.

Shechem, the son of Hamor the Hivite, was the prince of Edom. After Shechem saw Dinah, he took her and lay with her, violating her. He loved her and wanted to marry her. He asked his father to secure her as his wife. Hamor, Shechem's father, went to speak to Jacob about the matter. Jacob's sons came in and overheard the conversation. They were troubled and very angry because Shechem had violated their sister. Hamor tried to convince them that Shechem, his son, loved their sister. Shechem wanted to make it right by marrying Dinah. This way, the two families could dwell together in the same land in peace.

Jacob's sons Simeon and Levi agreed, but they specified one condition. The condition was that all male Shechemites submit to being circumcised—a Hebrew tradition of removing the foreskins of all males aged eight months or older. Hamor agreed. On the third day afterward, when the pain and soreness of circumcision was at its height and movement was difficult for the

Shechemites, Simeon and Levi attacked and slew all of the males in the city, including Shechem. They then plundered the city. They took the Shechemites' sheep, oxen, and donkeys; what was in the field and what was in the city; and all the wealth. All the little ones and the wives, they took captive.

Jacob was very grieved by this incident. Later, on his deathbed, he referred to it when prophesying a blessing on his sons Simeon and Levi (Genesis 49:5–7). Because of this incident, Jacob feared for his life and the life of his family. He was concerned that people of the surrounding tribes would kill them. God told him to go to Bethel and dwell there. "Make an altar there and call upon the name of the Lord and remember what I did for you before when you were in trouble." Jacob told his family to pack up and put away their gods. They did as instructed.

Had Dinah been content to remain close to her family, the terrible massacre that ensued may not have occurred.

How many young people today are hypnotized by the sights and sounds of the world? How many reject their family upbringing, leave home, and become lost in the excitements of the world? Some never return; others, like the Prodigal Son, may return broken and empty, thinking of to what heights they might have ascended had they never left.

"Children, obey your parents in the Lord, for this is right. Honor your father and mother, which is the first commandment with promise; that it may be well with you and you may live long on the earth" (Ephesians 6:1–3).

# TAMAR

*Genesis 38:6–30*

The Bible provides nothing about Tamar's background. It does say that Tamar was first married to Er, Judah's firstborn son who offended the Lord and died. (Judah was Jacob's fourth-born son. His mother's name was Leah.) She was then married to Er's younger brother Onan, who refused to beget children for his elder brother. For his offense, Onan also died. Judah had one more son, Shelah. Fearing that Shelah, his last seed, would also die, Judah insisted that Tamar return home to her parents until the boy became of age. But when Shelah became of age, Judah failed to keep his promise.

At that point, Tamar, twice married and twice widowed, and still childless, was desperate and devised a plan. She resorted to a dishonest method to accomplish her aim. Although I do not condone her method, I acknowledge that it involved two players playing the same game.

Judah's wife, Shuah, had died. He went to visit his friend Hirah, an Adullamite. Tamar set her trap to gain what had been denied her three times—a child. She removed her garments of widowhood, dressed herself as a prostitute, and sat beside the road to Timnath. She knew that Judah would be passing that way because it was sheep shearing time. Sure enough, along came Judah. Not recognizing Tamara as his daughter-in-law, he bargained for her favors and secured them. "What will thou give me?" she asked. He promised her a kid from the flock. She demanded a pledge until he sent the lamb. He gave her his signet ring, bracelets, and staff. Tamar returned to her home wearing her widow's garments.

When Judah later sent his servant with the promised kid from the flock, the servant could find no prostitute in that city.

About three months later, when it was discovered that Tamar was with child and the news reached Judah that his daughter-in-law had played the harlot, Judah self-righteously demanded that she be brought forth and burned on the cheek or forehead—and thereby branded as a harlot—which was the legal punishment for the sin of adultery. Judah schemed how to get rid of her so he would not have to give his last son, Shelah, to her to marry. When Tamar was brought before the judge and asked whose child she was carrying, she presented Judah's ring, bracelet, and staff and stated with confidence that the father of her child was the man who owned those objects. "By the man whose these are I am with child," she said. Judah's jaws dropped. While still in shock, Judah was provoked by his conscience, which compelled him to say out loud, "She has been more righteous than I, because I gave her not to Shelah my son to wed." The last part of Genesis 38:26 says, "And he knew her again no more," meaning that Judah never again had sexual relations with Tamar.

You might say that Judah was motivated in his sensual conduct by lust alone, but Tamar by a higher motive, namely, to become a mother which had been denied her three times. Twin sons were born of the incestuous relationship between Judah and Tamar. Their names were Perez and Zerah. Through Perez, Tamar became an ancestor of Jesus Christ (Matthew 1:3).

# ASENATH

*Genesis 41:45-50*

Asenath was the wife of Joseph and a daughter of Potiphera, who was priest of On, the national temple of the sun, or Heliopolis, a sacred city of sun worshipers. Before the famine, Pharaoh gave Asenath to Joseph to marry. She bore him two sons. The oldest was Manasses, meaning "to cause to forget," and the youngest was Ephraim, meaning "doubly fruitful."

These sons and their offspring were very well-known and played a vital role in the kingdom of Israel. Their grandfather Jacob blessed these grandsons along with Joseph and his eleven brothers. These two grandsons also became heads of tribes.

Some scholars suggest that Joseph's marriage to Asenath was a diplomatic arrangement, designated by Pharaoh to place him inside a strictly delineated, aristocratic society, and thus to convert him into a naturalized Egyptian citizen and cause him to forget his God. Was this act successful? There is no indication in the Bible that Joseph made a religious transition fitting this description. One tradition says that through Joseph's influence Asenath renounced her sun gods and became a worshiper of Jehovah God.

# PUAH AND SHIPHRAH

*Exodus 1:15-21*

After the death of Joseph and his entire generation, a new pharaoh came to the throne who knew not of Joseph. Even thou the Hebrews continued to be fruitful and multiply, the new king feared that one day, because of their number, they might think to overthrow the Egyptian empire. So the Egyptians implemented a plan to prevent this from happening. "Come let us deal shrewdly with them, lest they multiply, and it happen, in the event of war, that they also join our enemies and fight against us, and so go up out of the land" (Exodus 1:10).

"Then the king of Egypt spoke to the Hebrew midwives, of whom the name of one was Shiphrah and the name of the other Puah; and he said, 'When you do the duties of a midwife for the Hebrew women, and see them on the birthstools, if it is a son, then you shall kill him; but if it is a daughter, then she shall live'" (Exodus 1:15).

After receiving the king's command to commit murder, the two midwives named in the Scripture above were caught between a rock and a hard spot. Whom should they obey, the God of the Hebrews in whom they had come to believe, or the king? True to their conscience and calling, they knew that Pharaoh's directive conflicted with the divine command not to kill, and so they spared the boy children, thereby obeying God rather than a man.

The next verse says, "But they feared God." Even when Puah and Shiphrah knew that their lives were at stake, their minds were fixed on doing right, even in a heathen land. The Bible says that Puah and Shiphrah, whose names are Egyptian, were Hebrew midwives. So the king had asked Hebrews to murder Hebrews?

Aben Ezra, an historian of ancient Jewish culture, says that the two women were chiefs over all the midwives, who were more than five hundred. He also suggested that they were Egyptians who were married to Hebrews and had embraced the Hebrew faith, which giving them the status of being Hebrew.

Whomever Puah and Shiphrah were, they feared the Lord. And God used them as instruments to protect His people. When they feared God and honored Him by doing the right thing, God honored them and not only preserved their lives, but provided houses for them (1 Samuel 2:30).

# JOCHEBED

*Exodus 1; 2:1–11, 20*
*Numbers 26:59*

Jochebed is the most renowned of all Hebrew mothers because of the great part she played in helping to fulfill God's plan to Abraham. Jochebed was married to Amram. They were both of the house of Levi. Jochebed was both wife and aunt of Amram. She was Amran's father's sister (Exodus 6:20).

Jacob and his family numbered seventy when they arrived in Egypt. They were assigned to the community of Goshen. They grew and waxed strong. Joseph eventually died. The pharaoh who knew Joseph also died. After that, another pharaoh came to the throne, one who did not look with favor upon the Hebrews. As a matter of fact, he feared them lest they should someday outnumber the Egyptians and take over the nation. He set over them taskmasters to afflict them with great burdens. But the greater their affliction, the greater their growth. Thus, he commanded that the midwives, Shiphrah and Puah, who were the overseers of the midwives,, destroy all the boys at birth and save only the girls. But the midwives were God-fearing and did not as Pharaoh commanded, but kept the male children alive also. When that didn't happen, he commanded that all newborn Hebrew boys be thrown into the Nile River.

At the time of this law, Jochebed was heavy with child. She and Amran had two children already: Miriam, about nine years old, and Aaron, perhaps three. The thought of her baby being a male child and being destroyed terrified Jochebed, so she and Amran turned to God in faith and supplication. God gave Jochebed a marvelous and ingenious plan once her third child was born. Jochebed kept the infant in her home as long as she could, until his cries were too loud and she feared he would be heard by Pharaoh's guards.

Jochebed made a basket of straw and pitch, light enough to allow it to float on the water, and placed Moses in the basket, with his sister, Miriam, watching nearby. The plan worked. In a way, Jochebed complied with the law to put her baby in the river. She just made sure he floated instead of drown.

When Pharaoh's daughter came to the river to bathe, as her custom was, she heard the baby crying and commanded her maid to bring the basket to her. When she saw the beautiful baby boy, her heart was deeply touched. She decided that she needed a maid to care for this beautiful Hebrew baby. Miriam came out of hiding and volunteered to find a maid. She chose her mother, of course. Are we to assume that Jochebed agreed to nurse her own precious child for the princess? No, her motive was something different: to train her child for the great calling for which he was born. She was working for God and not for the princess. This mother had a sincere conviction that she must give account to God for this child. God had great plans for Moses. He was born for a great work. He was entrusted to God-fearing parents. He was placed in a home whose parents were willing to accept the responsibility.

Jochebed was a faithful mother. She mothered and trained one of the greatest leaders who ever lived on this earth. Moses's education began at home, with his mother as his teacher. She did a thorough job until he went away to be trained in the wisdom of the Egyptians.

As Pharaoh's heir, Moses stood true to the teaching of his mother. The writer of Hebrews 11 says, "He chose rather to suffer affliction with the people of God than to enjoy the pleasures of sin for a season, esteeming the reproach of Christ greater riches than the treasures in Egypt."

It cannot be overemphasized how important a child's formative years (ages one to seven) are. These are the years when children's minds are like sponges that soak up every influence they are exposed to, negative or positive. The historical records indicate that by the time Moses was between the ages of seven and twelve, Jochebed was off the scene and out of Moses's life. But just look at how much she accomplished in those short years. What a challenge to all mothers everywhere!

Amram and Jochebed, as stated previously, had three children. They all became preeminent in the leadership of Israel.

1. Moses, the great emancipator and law-giver

2. Aaron, Israel's first high priest

3. Miriam, the prophetess, poet, and musician

These three offspring stayed with God. Although they had their shortcomings, they never left the Faith. Raising three God-fearing children is one of the highest achievements a parent can accomplish in this life.

# ZIPPORAH

*Exodus 2:21; 4:24-26*
*Numbers 12*

Zipporah was the oldest of seven daughters of Jethro, or Reuel, the priest of Midian. She became the wife of Moses, the national hero who delivered the Israelites from Egyptian slavery, established them as an independent nation, and prepared them for entering Canaan.

Zipporah gave Moses two fine sons, Gershom and Eliezer. Not much is written in Scripture about Gershom and Eliezer. In Exodus 4:24–26, it is recounted that Zipporah saved Moses's life from the vengeance of the Lord by circumcising his son with a sharp stone. Scripture does not indicate which son was circumcised.

> Though called a "Cushite woman" in Numbers 12:1, the wife of Moses was a Midianite, and thus a descendant of Abraham. In personal appearance, she differed from the Hebrews in being of a somewhat darker complexion. Though not an Israelite, Zipporah was a worshiper of the true God. She was of a timid, retiring disposition, gentle and affectionate, and greatly distressed at the sight of suffering; and it was for this reason that Moses, when on the way to Egypt, had

consented to her return to Midian. He desired to spare her the pain of witnessing the judgments that were to fall on the Egyptians.[1]

In Numbers 12, Moses is criticized for having married Zipporah the Cushite. It was Moses's sister, Miriam, who led their brother Aaron to criticize Moses. But neither Zipporah nor Moses tried to rebut Miriam. In Romans 12: 17–1, God says, "Vengeance is Mine ... I will repay." And that He did. Leprosy came upon Miriam, and she became as white as snow. Aaron pleaded with Moses to intercede with God on Miriam's behalf. Moses did as requested. God heard his prayer. Miriam was miraculously healed after she was shut outside the camp for seven days, per the Mosaic health laws.

Zipporah is a Midian name meaning a "little bird" such as a sparrow. Usually Biblical names were indicative of the person's character or destiny. Her participation and involvement were perhaps limited by her quiet and unassuming personality.

---

[1]    Ellen White, *Patriarchs and Prophets* (Coldwater, Michigan: Remnant Publications, 1997), 400.

# MIRIAM

*Exodus 2:1–8; 15:1, 21*
*Numbers 12*

Miriam, the sister of Moses, is called a prophetess in Exodus 15:1 and 15:21. She is the same Miriam who hid in the bushes to watch over Moses as he floated in the Nile River when Pharaoh's daughter came with her servants for her daily bath (Exodus 4:1–10). Miriam was very quick in saying to Pharaoh's daughter that she could find a nursemaid for the baby. She saved her brother and thereby allowed him to be brought up by his mother, which was part of God's plan.

We see Miriam the second time when she is in her old age. She had been chosen by God, along with her brother Aaron, to assist Moses in leading the children of Israel out of bondage. Moses was the appointed leader, but his direct dealings would have been primarily with the men, who were considered the heads of their families. Miriam's task was, perhaps, to lead the women. One might consider Miriam to be the first women's ministry leader, for the Scripture says of her, "Then Miriam the prophetess ... took up a timbrel in her hand and all the women went out after her with timbrels and dances. Then she led out in the song, 'Sing ye to the Lord, for He has triumphed gloriously, the horse and his rider He has thrown into the sea.'" Miriam was indeed a leader.

With much uncertainty facing the group of Israelites as they were about to embark on an experience they'd never had before, Miriam knew they needed spiritual motivation to undertake the journey out of Egypt. She could see anxiety in their faces. As a gifted leader, she knew that a cheerful song with encouraging words was one of the best ways to lift the dirge of apprehension.

The third time we see Miriam, the defects in her character come into clear focus when her feelings about Moses's Ethiopian wife are revealed (Numbers 12). Miriam said, "Has the Lord indeed spoken only through Moses? Has He not spoken through us also?" And the Lord heard it. It was she who brought the matter to Aaron and influenced his thinking. Then she made her complaint public. That was her big mistake. She should have requested a private audience with Moses instead.

Leadership should not go against leadership, especially in public. It tends to break down the authority and respect of the appointed leader and also jeopardizes the hope of the people. God struck Miriam with leprosy. This devastating plague of Egypt regarded as providential punishment for sin had smitten Miriam. She had become a leper, white as snow. And Moses cried unto the Lord to heal her. Though Miriam had held a grudge against her younger brother, Moses acted toward her with a spirit of love and forgiveness. We can assume that Miriam was touched by her brother's love. She was shut out of the camp for seven days in accordance with the health law regulations of the Israelites. She was later returned to the group and her position. Not until then did the group move forward.

While the children of Israel were encamped in Kadesh, in the desert of Zin, Miriam died at an old age and was buried there (Numbers 20:1).

According to Flavius Josephus, Miriam married Hur, who, together with Aaron, had held up Moses's arms in the battle with the Amalekites.[1]

"For whosoever exalteth himself shall be abased and he that humbleth himself shall be exalted" (Luke 14:11).

---

[1]    *The Works of Josephus* (Philadelphia: David McKay Publisher, 1878), 98.

# ELISHEBA

*Exodus 6:23*
*Numbers 2:3*

Elisheba is the Hebrew form of the name Elizabeth.

Elisheba was the daughter of Amminadab. Her brother was Naashon, a captain in the tribe of Judah. Elisheba was married to Aaron, who was the first high priest and also the older brother of Moses.

To this couple were born four sons: Nadab, Abihu, Eleazar, and Ithamar. Elisheba's and Aaron's two oldest sons, Nadab and Abihu, were killed by God for offering strange fire while making sacrifices in the temple.

Elisheba's grandson Phinehas, the son of Eleazar, succeeded his father as the next high priest. Moses, directed by God, granted Phinehas a covenant of peace for his bold act of taking his javelin and piercing it through Zimri, chief among the Simeonites, and Cozbi, a princess of Median, which stayed the hand of God in the plague that was brought upon Israel in the "apostasy at the border." The covenant named an everlasting priesthood for Phinehas and all of his descendants.

Elisheba's father and brother are listed in the genealogy of Jesus Christ. Therefore, it would be logical to assume that Elisheba was also of the tribe of Judah.

# COZBI

*Numbers 25, 31*

During the time of the Israelites' sojourn in Canaan, they camped at Shittim, on the border of Midianite country. The leader of that country, Balak, offered to pay Balaam (a supposedly godly prophet) to curse the Israelites. For the love of money, Balaam tried two times to inflict the curse, but God would not permit him to curse the Israelites. This bespeaks of God's love and protection. If you abide under the shadow of the Almighty, then you will be protected. " No weapon formed against you shall prosper (Isaiah 54:17).

When his first and second attempts failed, Balaam advised the Midianites to have a feast to honor their god, Baalpeor, and invite the Israelites to it. Once they received the invitation, the Israelites thought, *Can't hurt to go and just observe.* At the feast, where they were hypnotized with music, dancing, food, and sex, the Israelites forgot their loyalty to Jehovah God.

Cozbi was a Midianite princess, the daughter of Zur, who was the head of a chief house in Midian. Although a princess, Cozbi had an evil influence on the people. Hers is the only female name listed in the recounting of the feast that led to the moral and religious corruption of the nation of Israel. The Bible record indicates that twenty-four thousand died in the plague and some twenty-three thousand died in war.

Phinehas, the son of High Priest Eleazar, filled to the brim with righteous indignation and holy boldness, picked up a javelin and pierced through Zimri and Cozbi with a sword while they were still engaged in their sensual act of reveling. As a result, God stayed the plague and did not destroy the nation of Israel that day.

"The greatest want of the world is the want of men—men who will not be bought or sold; men who in their inmost souls are true and honest; men who do not fear to call sin by its right name; men whose conscience is as true to duty as the needle to the pole; men who will stand for the right though the heavens fall."[1]

As for Cozbi, "For the lips of an immoral woman drip honey, and her mouth is smoother than oil; but in the end she is bitter as wormwood, sharp as a two-edged sword. Her feet go down to death, her steps lay hold of hell" (Proverbs 5:3–5).

---

[1]     Ellen White, *Education.*

# ZELOPHEDAD'S FIVE DAUGHTERS; MAHLAH, NOAH, HOGLAH, MILCAH, AND TUGAH

*Numbers 27:1–11*

In a time when Moses's civil laws, which were given to him directly by God, governed the Hebrew nation, especially during the Israelites' sojourn from Egypt to the Promised Land, one of these laws stated that women did not inherit land. Only the males or sons in the family inherited the family's land. A daughter would become a part of her husband's family.

There was a man named Zelophehad. Of the tribe of Manasseh, he was one of Joseph's sons. This man had no sons, but he did have five daughters. When Zelophehad died, his portion of land, according to law, would return to the family, to his siblings. His daughters, who were still single, would get nothing. This is one of the reasons that men always wanted to have at least one son, to perpetuate their name and their legacy.

Zelophehad's daughters analyzed their situation and counseled together. After that, they went to Moses to petition him about rights they didn't possess under the present law. Moses listened. This was a situation he had not encountered before. So he took their cause before the Lord. God authorized Moses to amend the civil laws so that the daughters of Zelophehad could retain their father's property, with one condition: they must marry within their own tribe.

I conclude that these women's speaking up for themselves was not happenstance. Instead, it was the result of their focused and purposeful characters. They were not just "silly girls." They had applied themselves to acquiring knowledge through reading, listening, and observing; they had made themselves aware of the laws of the land; they were in the know. When their father, the patriarch, was deceased, they analyzed their situation and, after much prayer, seized the opportunity to go straight to Moses, the earthly authority on the law, knowing that he would then appeal to the heavenly authority. After doing this, the women saw a positive result.

They set a precedent. The real-estate laws today in most states are very similar to those implemented by Moses and influenced by the daughters of Zelophehad millennia ago, with one exception: today, there are no restrictions on whom a woman marries after she receives an inheritance of land.

This is an exemplary story. In a patriarchal (male-dominated) society, these five women stood up against inequality and won. Remember, when you are justified in your heart, motive, and actions, your prayers can move the hand of God. Zelophehad's daughters did just that!

# RAHAB

*Joshua 1*

Jericho was the worst of the Amorites' cities. God instructed Joshua to destroy the city and its inhabitants. Rahab, a harlot, lived in Jericho. From her unsavory clients, she heard stories about the Israelite conquest from time to time: the crossing of the Red Sea, the crossing of the Jordan River, etc. Having not seen these events, she merely heard of them—and believed.

When Joshua sent two spies to survey Jericho, they providentially arrived at Rahab's house, which was one of the houses on top of the city wall. The spies had already been spotted by the king's posse, so they were looking for a place to hide. Being the industrious woman that she was, even though a harlot, Rahab began to negotiated with the spies, saying that she would ensure their safety if the people in her household/family would be rescued and allowed to live when the city was overthrown. Perhaps Rahab's mother and sisters, who were no doubt in the same profession, were included in the agreement.

Having settled the matter, Rahab proceeded to hide the spies. When the posse came by, she denied that the two men were there. When Rahab and the spies considered it safe, she held a scarlet cord while they lowered themselves down the outside wall.

When Joshua took the city, all of its inhabitants, apart from Rahab and her family, were destroyed. A piece of scarlet cord hanging from Rahab's window was the identifier of her residence.

What Rahab " was is not as important as what she" became". Many Bible characters were far from perfect, but, through determination and grace, they were able to rise above and overcome their defects of character. Rahab was one of these people. She was numbered with those upon whom Jesus pronounced a blessing for their belief although they had not seen, yet they believed (John 20:29). Rahab's actions that day secured her a place in the hall of faith mentioned in the eleventh chapter of Hebrews. In the great hall of faith in Hebrews 11, Rahab is listed among the faithful. In James 2:25-26, James deems her worthy because of her works. She is commended for her faith and for her works. Whatever she might have been or done, she did overcome and was forgiven.

Thus, Rahab is one of the four non-Jewish women listed in the genealogy of Jesus Christ (Matthew 1), the four being Tamar, Rahab, Ruth, and Beersheba (the wife of Uriah).

"Though your sins be as scarlet, they shall be as white as snow, though they be red like crimson, they shall be as wool" (Isaiah 1:18).

# ACHSAH

*Joshua 15:16–19*
*Judges 1:12–15*
*1 Chronicles 2:4, 9*

Achsah was the only daughter of Caleb, who was a prince of the tribe of Judah and the senior statesman of the Hebrew nation. Caleb had three sons. Achsah was perhaps a bit spoiled. Caleb and Joshua became distinguished when, under Moses's leadership, they were chosen to be among the twelve spies who were to spy out the land of Canaan before the Israelites crossed over the Jordan River to enter the Promised Land. Caleb and Joshua were the only two who had faith enough to believe that they could conquer the land.

When Achsah's story begins, Joshua is dead and Caleb is an old warrior. Caleb had received his share in the division of the land. He had fought and won many battles. There was one territory in Canaan that was very difficult to conquer, so he gave a challenge to the young men in the camp: whoever could conquer and capture Kiriath-Sepher would receive his daughter, Achsah, as a prize. The winner was Othniel, son of Kenaz, Caleb's younger brother. Thus, Achsah became the wife of her first cousin.

Achsah was given a sufficient dowry of land. But she asked for more, which included the upper and lower springs. Some scholars suggest that this was a sign of her selfishness. I submit that perhaps she knew that water was needed to water the land or else the land might have been useless. Caleb granted her request.

When the children of Israel did evil in the sight of the Lord, the Lord became angry and sold them into the hand of the man with the iron chariots, Cushan-Rishathaim, King of Mesopotamia. The Israelites served this king for eight hard years. When they cried out to God, the Lord raised up a deliverer to deliver them. The Spirit of the Lord came upon Othniel, and he delivered God's people. Othniel judged Israel for forty years.

Thus, Achsah was honored to be the wife of the first of fifteen judges who judged Israel over a period of 350 to 400 years. The first was Othniel; the last, Samuel. See appendix A, "Chart of Hebrew Judges."

# DEBORAH

*Judges 4-5*

The name Deborah means "bee," which is indicative of Deborah's character. The wife of Lapidoth and the fourth judge of Israel in the days of the judges, Deborah was industrious, patient, determined, and faithful. She was also a prophetess, a warrior, and a great spiritual motivator. Deborah is one of several females in Scripture considered to have a prophetic gift: the ability to discern the deep messages of and will of God and communicate or teach these to others.

When Ehud (the previous judge) was dead, the children of Israel again did evil in the sight of the Lord, as was their habit of doing things. So the Lord sold them into the hand of Jabin, King of Canaan. The commander of Jabin's army was Sisera. The children of Israel feared Sisera because he had nine hundred chariots of iron. For twenty years, he had oppressed them. So they cried out to the Lord, who heard their cries.

Then arose Deborah, a mother of Israel (Judges 5:7). There is no record of Deborah's being a natural mother. Evidently, she possessed motherly traits: she was caring, tender, patient, helpful, and compassionate, and she had the ability to give good, sound spiritual counsel. Evidently, she also knew the law and could decipher it correctly in judging the Israelite nation. No woman had ever held such a position before; neither did any women judges come after Deborah. The position of women in Deborah's day was subordinate to men, but Deborah lifted women to a higher plain. Deborah's position as a leader of Israel was quite remarkable.

The palm tree under which Deborah ruled and possibly lived was a landmark, as palms were rare in Palestine at the time. In honor of her works, the palm became known as "the palm of Deborah."

Deborah did more than judge (counsel). She also roused the nation from its lethargy and despair. Day after day, she encouraged those who gathered to hear her words of divine wisdom by discussing the certainty of their deliverance from their heathen foe. If only they would repent and trust in God, they could overcome their fear and their foe.

God made known His will to Deborah. She sent for General Barak, the son of Abinoam of Naphtali, and told him that it was God's will that he should lead her forces. She also told him that God would deliver the country. Barak was a great general, but, because of his knowledge of the number and strength of his opponent, he was apprehensive. He said to Deborah, "If thou wilt go with me I will go: but if thou wilt not go with me then I will not go." Deborah said, "I will surely go with thee, notwithstanding the journey that thou takest shall not be for thine honor; for the lord shall sell Sisera, Jaban's military leader, into the hand of a woman." This brave-hearted and fearless leader went into physical battle. It wasn't just words anymore. It was God's battle, and God was on Deborah's side.

The odds were seemingly insurmountable. Sisera commanded a hundred thousand soldiers and had nine hundred iron chariots. Barak had only ten thousand men from the tribes of Napali and Zebelon. Some others had been summoned, but these either could not come or refused to come because of fear.

God fought against Sisera. A great hailstorm came upon the battlefield. The Canaanites were blinded by the rain, and the swollen River Kishon washed them away. The Lord routed Sisera, his chariots, and his entire army to the edge of the swords held by Barak and his army.. All of the foes except Sisera were killed. Sisera's chariot became stuck in the mud. Sisera jumped from his chariot and fled away on foot. He fled to the tent of Herber, his friend. Heber was not at home. He was met by Heber's wife, Jael, who took him in and offered him kind hospitality. After he had relaxed and fallen asleep, Jael took a tent peg and killed Sisera with it. What Deborah the prophetess had said came true. One of the identifying marks of a true prophetess/prophet is that everything they prophesy must come true, not merely a part, of what he or she prophesies, but all.

Deborah was also a writer and singer. Her poem of praise about this victory in battle makes up the entire fifth chapter of Judges. I suggest you read it.

# JAEL, THE DELIVERER OF ISRAEL

*Judges 4:9; 17–24*

Jael was the wife of Heber the Kenite, who had cut himself off from his people. Neutral in his relationship with any country, Heber was a blacksmith by trade. This would explain his friendly relationship with Jabin, the Canaanite king, as he was undoubtedly the builder of Jabin's nine hundred chariots of iron.

During the battle between the Israelites and the Canaanites, God intervened and unleashed the powers of nature, completely disorganizing Jabin's army. They were all killed by the storm or the Israelites' swords, all except Sisera, captain of the army. His chariot was stuck in the mud. So he fled on foot to the nearest safe place, or so he thought: the tent of his friend Heber the Kenite. Evidently, Heber was not at home. Heber's wife met Sisera at the door and invited him in. When he requested water, she gave him milk. She made him comfortable and covered him up. Weary from the battle, he fell into a deep sleep.

Then Jael took a tent peg and a hammer in her hand and went quietly to Sisera. She drove the peg into his temple. The peg went through his head and down into the ground, for Sisera was fast asleep. He died. When Barak came pursuing him, Jael said to him, "I will show you the man whom you seek." When Barak went into her tent, he saw Sisera lying there dead with the peg in his temple.

God can and will use anybody who will permit Him. Jael was not of Israel. She was the wife of Heber the Kenite, who was offsprings of Ho'bab, Moses's father-in-law. Jael had audacity. We may question her method and her motive, but we must admit that she was a courageous woman. She was the instrument used by God to destroy the last man of the Canaanite army and put an end to approximately two decades of harassment, threats and intimidation by Jabin, king of the Canaanite nation.

Jael, I repeat, was courageous. Although her actions may be considered less than honorable, she did not plead neutrality. She took a stand—a stand with God's people—and made her statement loud and clear......... God was the winner that day!

Jael assassinated Sisera, the captain of Jabin's army. "So God subdued on that day Jabin the king of Canaan before the children of Israel ... until they had destroyed Jabin, king of Canaan by the hand of Jael, a woman" (Judges 4:23–24).

"Blessed among women is Jael, the wife of Heber the Kenite" (Judges 5:24).

# PENINNAH

*1 Samuel 1:2–6*

Peninnah was the second wife of Elkanah. Perhaps Elkanah married Peninnah because his first wife, Hannah, who was his favorite, was unable to bear children. Part of the cultural thinking in biblical times was that the primary purpose of a woman was to bear children. If a woman could not do that, then people believed that she had been frowned upon by God and that she was, therefore, useless.

Peninnah was Hannah's nemesis. The former harassed the latter constantly about her inability to bear a child. This was especially annoying when the two women went to Shiloh to worship because Peninnah harassed Hannah openly. Peninnah had many children, and each one of them received a portion of meat when Elkanah made an animal sacrifice at Shiloh. At these times, Elkanah gave a double portion of meat to Hannah, as he was trying to compensate for her lack of children. To Peninnah, this showed her husband's favoritism for Hannah, which led the former to harass the latter even more.

What can we learn from Peninnah? Some would say that we can learn nothing from her. But I suggest that as a result of Peninnah's constant provoking of Hannah, Hannah's faith became stronger. Hannah prayed to God and eventually prevailed over her rival. She gave birth to Samuel, who became a priest and a great prophet. She also gave birth to five other children: three sons and two daughters. Their names are not mentioned in Scripture. In Hannah's situation, we see how God can turn stumbling blocks into stepping-stones.

Scripture is silent about Peninnah's ancestry (i.e., her beginnings) and her end. Nothing remarkable is recorded about her life. She was the mother of many children, but, because of her jealousy and harassment of Hannah, she showed evidence of being an empty woman.

# HANNAH

*1 Samuel 1–2*

Hannah's name means "grace." I think that is appropriate for a woman who experienced such deep agony before experiencing such great ecstasy.

Hannah was the first of the two wives of Elkanah. The second wife was Peninnah. Hannah was barren, which, perhaps, is the reason her husband took another wife. Elkanah's second marriage was the beginning of Hannah's sorrow. If a woman who lived in biblical times could not bear children, she was considered to have God's disfavor.

Peninnah provoked Hannah constantly. As a result of this harassment, Hannah's countenance was depressed most of the time. Elkanah was a godly man who always took his family with him when he went to the yearly feast at Shiloh to worship. When he made animal sacrifices, he always gave double portions of meat to Hannah, and regular portions to Peninnah and her children. This was to compensate for Hannah's lack of children, but it only made matters worse.

On one occasion at a feast, Peninnah provoked Hannah so severely that the latter cried and refused to eat. Her husband said to her, "Hannah, why do you not eat? And why is your heart grieved? Am I not better to you than ten sons" (1 Samuel 1:8)?

One year at the Shiloh feast, Hannah's spirit was very deeply grieved. She prayed to the Lord, weeping in anguish. Then she made a vow, saying, "O Lord of hosts, if You will indeed look on the affliction of Your maidservant and remember me, and not forget Your maidservant, but will give Your maidservant a male child, then I will give him to the Lord all the days of his life, and no razor shall come upon his head" (1 Samuel 1:10–11). Eli the priest was sitting by the door. Seeing Hannah crying and noticing that her lips were moving, Eli assumed she was drunk. Hannah was not drunk. She was praying in her heart. Still, Eli admonished her and accused her of being drunk.

Hannah corrected him by saying, "I have drunk neither wine nor intoxicating drink, but poured out my soul before the Lord."

Eli replied, "Go in peace and the Lord God of Israel grant you the petition which you have asked."

The next year, Hannah conceived and gave birth to a son, whom she named Samuel (meaning, "asked of God"), because she had asked for him from the Lord. She chose not to attend the feast that year. She explained to her husband that she wanted to wean the child first. After the boy was weaned, she would take him to Shiloh so that he may appear before the Lord and remain there forever. Just as Sarah prayed for Isaac and just as Rachel prayed for Joseph, Hannah prayed for Samuel. Prayer works as well now as it did then.

When Samuel was weaned, Hannah, as she had promised, took him along to Shiloh for the customary sacrificial offering to the Lord. There, she said to Eli, "O my lord! As your soul lives, my lord, I am the woman who stood by you here, praying to the Lord. For I prayed, and the Lord has granted me my petition which I asked of Him. Therefore I also have lent him to the Lord as long as he lives he shall be lent to the Lord."

In motherhood, Hannah found her greatest fulfillment. Hannah was humble, trusting, and committed. When she wanted a son, she honestly prayed for one— and God answered her prayer. Hannah had made a vow and kept it. How tempting it must have been for her to forget that vow. She was patient, prayerful, faithful, meek, and full of spiritual devotion and motherly love. Her heart was true.

When we honor God, He honors us. First Samuel 2:21 tells us that Hannah went on to have three more sons and two daughters, whose names are not listed in Scripture. In the course of time, Samuel went on to become a towering figure in Israel. He was the last judge of Israel as well as a priest. He anointed Saul as the first king of Israel. And while Saul was still on the throne, God commanded him to anoint David, who was but a lad at that time, as king.

Hannah must have understood the importance of Samuel's early childhood. It is in the childhood years when 90 percent of a person's personality is formed. In her son's formative years, Hannah prepared Samuel for his high calling—a lifetime of service to God—for which she had consecrated him before he was born.

John MacArthur wrote the following about Hannah:

"Hannah is a reminder that mothers are the makers of men and the architects of the next generation Hannah's love for her husband

and devotion to God is the first key to understanding her profound influence as a mother. The love between husband and wife is the real key to a thriving family. A healthy home environment cannot be built exclusively on the parents' love for their children. The properly situated family has marriage at the center; families shouldn't revolve only around the children. Furthermore, all parents need to heed this lesson: what you communicate to your children through your marital relationship will stay with them for the rest of their lives. By watching how mother and father treat one another, they will learn the most fundamental lessons of life; love, self-sacrifice, integrity, virtue, sin, compassion, and forgiveness. Whatever you teach them about those things, right or wrong, is planted deep within their hearts".

The following is true of Hannah: "Who can find a virtuous woman? For her price is far above rubies. ... She looketh well to the ways of her household, and eateth not the bread of idleness. ... Her children arise up and call her blessed; her husband also and he praiseth her" (Proverbs 31:10, 27, 28).

# AHINOAM

*1 Samuel 14:49–50; 31:2*
*1 Chronicles 8:33*

Ahinoam, whose father's name was Ahimaaz, was the wife of King Saul. Nothing is known about her character. She bore five children for King Saul. Although Saul, in 1 Chronicles, is said to have had another son (Abinadab), perhaps that child was born to another of Saul's wives. Ahinoam had two girls and three boys. The daughters were named Merab (the older) and Michal (the younger). The sons were named Jonathan, Isha (which is short for Ishbaal or Ishbosheth), and Melchisua.

It appears that Merab died young and that Michal raised her sisters five sons as her own. Merab was first promised to David in marriage, but later she was given to Adriel. Then, because Michal loved David, Michal was given to David to marry. This marriage was of short duration. When David had to flee for his life, he left Michal with her parents. Although still legally married to David, she was given to another, Phalti, in marriage. When David returned some ten years later, he sent for Michal. Thereafter, she was restored as his wife.

Jonathan, Abinadab, and Melchisua were killed in battle along with their father.

Ishbosheth became a puppet king. When he and Abner, his uncle who was Saul's military general and now his, had a dispute, this caused Abner to leave Ishbosheth and to join with David. Ishbosheth became faint-hearted and deserted his throne, running for his life.

It must have been a real challenge for Ahinoam to be the wife of a man who experienced many different changes in mood. Ahinoam was, no doubt, a woman of deep and abiding faith. She had to be in order to contend with her husband's temperament and many moods. (King Saul seems to have suffered from a combination of bipolar disorder, manic depression, paranoia, and schizophrenia. He was a man who had no peace).

Scripture is silent about what happened to Ahinoam after Saul died.

# MERAB

*1 Samuel 14:49; 18:17, 19*

Merab was the oldest of five siblings: Merab, Michal, Jonathan, Isha (or Ishbosheth), and Melchisua. Her mother was Ahinoam, one of King Saul's wives. King Saul, therefore, was Merab's father.

Merab's father had promised David that he would give Merab to be his wife if David avenged the Israelites by defeating the Philistines. Because Saul was jealous of David, he hoped that David would be killed in battle. After David accomplished the mission, King Saul conveniently forgot his promise. Instead of giving Merab to David, he gave her to Adriel the Meholathite, the son of Barzillai, to marry. To their union were born five sons whose names are not mentioned in Scripture. The Scriptures make the allusion that Merab died prematurely. Her sister, Michal, raised her children. Thank God for sisters!

# MICHAL

*1 Samuel 14:49; 18:20–28; 19:11–17*
*2 Samuel 3:13, 14; 6:16–23; 21:8*
*Chronicles 15:29*

Michal was the second of five children: Merab, Michal, Jonathan, Ishbosheth, and Melchisua. King Saul was her father, and Ahinoam was her mother.

Michal's older sister, Merab, was promised to David in marriage, but Merab was given to Adriel instead. Michal loved David and made no effort to conceal her love for this highly honored hero of Israel. Saul's jealousy of David caused him to devise means whereby David would be slain by the Philistines. King Saul asked David to return with a hundred Philistine foreskins as a dowry for his daughter. What a strange request. David presented Saul with two hundred Philistine foreskins instead. And King Saul was forced to keep his word. Yet King Saul was bent on destroying David. He sent messengers to slay David in his house. Michal suspected something and helped David escape through a window. After all, she was the daughter of a trickster. When her father enquired why she did this, her response was that David had threatened to kill her.

It was many years later when Michal saw David again. After her father and her brother had been killed, and after David had reigned for seven years as king in Hebron, David relocated to

Jerusalem along with the six other wives he had acquired while he had been hiding from Michal's father in Hebron.

When David was established in Jerusalem, he evoked his kingly authority and sent for his first wife, Michal. They had not divorced, so she was still his wife, although she had been given to another by her father. David and Michal, although they had been married for several years, had no children. Michal's husband Phalti was very distraught when Michal was ordered to return to David. He followed behind her, weeping, until the mighty Abner demanded that he go back.

David truly loved the Lord. He also loved Michal. One day, as David and his assistants were bringing the ark of the covenant, the symbol of Jehovah's presence, to Morea, he became so joyful that he stripped himself of his royal robe and danced before the Lord with all his might. Michal was watching from a window. For this act, she despised him in her heart. All the love she had for him turned to scorn. When he returned home, she said, "How glorious was the king today who uncovered himself in the eyes of the handmaids of his servants as one of the vain fellows shamelessly uncovers himself." Her lack of sensitivity and respect for what her husband represented is revealed in the foregoing statement. David was not expecting to hear such a thing from his wife, but he made it very clear that he was not ashamed of what he had done before the Lord. He reminded Michal that the Lord had chosen him, instead of any member of King Saul's family, to reign as king. (That was a direct put down to Michal and her family).

After David made this statement, we read in the Bible that Michal, the daughter of King Saul, died childless, which suggests that she lived apart from David from that time forward.

Because of the order in which these two statements appear in Scripture, scholars have assumed that the former was the reason for the latter—and maybe that is the case. But let us look a little into Michal's situation. Let's walk a mile in her shoes, if you will, and then decide what we would do under these circumstances:

Michal was married at an early age to the love of her life (David).

She was faithful to her husband and stood between him and her father.

She put her life in jeopardy to save her husband David by letting him down through the window.

She was pawned off to another man by her father. Her father was killed in battle.

Her brothers, Jonathan, Abinadab, and Melchisua, were also killed in battle.

Her only sister, Merab, died at an early age.

She raised her sister's five sons as if they were her own.

Her husband David was away for many years, during which time there was no communication from him.

David returned and tore Michal away from her second husband as if she were a pawn to be played with. He neither considered her emotions nor gave her a choice. No doubt, she had some feelings for her second husband after years of being married to him.

One of her brothers, Isha (or Ishbosheth), the puppet king, deserted the throne in fear of David after Abner, his uncle and military leader, left him and joined up with David. Nothing is said about what happened to Isha after that.

Michal's nephew Mephibosheth, Jonathan's crippled son, had been assassinated by two deserters of Saul's army.

When Michal was with David before he fled for Hebron, she had him all to herself—all of his time and affections. Later, she shared him with at least six other wives and many concubines. Her only marital experience had been with men with only one wife and that was her preference.

In addition to this, the five guiltless sons of Merab, which she had raised as her own for her sister, had been executed merciless by David's command to atone for her father's misdeeds. (See the story under the chapter "Rizpah).

Rizpah's two sons, who were Michal's half-brothers, were killed.

Where Michal's mother was, Scripture does not say. She was probably somewhere else, grieving for herself.

I submit to you that Michal's remarks in 2 Samuel 6: 19–20 represent only the tip of the iceberg. She was helpless and in a pathetic predicament, experiencing grief, feeling distraught, and being drained of all emotion. Even though she was married to the illustrious King David, she was at her wits' end, ready to explode. She perhaps thought as Naomi was thinking when she said, "Call me no more Naomi (Michal), but Mara, for God had dealt bitterly with me."

She was a broken woman.

# ABIGAIL (DAVID'S WIFE)

*1 Samuel 25:1–42*

On one occasion when David was a fugitive from King Saul, he was camped in Paran with his six hundred soldiers. There was a wealthy man in nearby Maon whose livestock were kept in Carmel. David and his men guarded the livestock voluntarily. The man's name was Nabal, which means "fool." His wife's name was Abigail, meaning "whose father is joy." On many occasions, David had guarded the herdsmen and the sheep. At sheep-shearing time, David sent men to Nabal to request some food. Nabal refused, treating David as any other vagabond. David became very angry. He armed himself and four hundred of his men so they could retaliate. God intervened through Nabal's quick-thinking, kind, and thoughtful wife, who had been informed of the incident by a loyal servant. She instructed her servant to saddle her donkey. Without delay, she—as perhaps she had done many times before to save her foolish drunkard husband—gathered food and wine and then called her servants. She took the food and wine to the king and apologetically pleaded for forgiveness for her husband. David accepted her apology and the food. When Abigail returned home, she found that her husband was having another drunken feast. She dared not tell him until the morning what she had done. Once she did tell him, he had a heart attack (or a stroke) and died ten days later. When David heard about Nabal's death and Abigail's fate, he sent for Abigail and made her his wife. Thus, Nabal's wife became David's wife.

The following is true of Abigail: "Who can find a virtuous woman? For her price is far above rubies. … She is like the merchant ship, she brings her food from afar. … She girds herself with strength and strengthens her arms. … She extends her hand to the poor, yea, she reaches out her hand to the needy. … Strength and honor are her clothing; she shall rejoice in times to come" (Proverbs 31:10, 14, 17, 20, 25).

# TAMAR (2)

*2 Samuel 13:1–32*
*1 Chronicles 3:9*

Tamar was the daughter of King David and Maacah. She was the sister of Absalom and the half-sister of Amnon, King David's son by Ahinoam, one of David's wives.

Amnon, King David's oldest son, fell in love with his half-sister Tamar. Instead of asking for her hand in marriage, which would have been acceptable in biblical times, he listened to his first cousin, Jonadab, who encouraged him to seduce her against her will. Given Amnon's immature character, he set up a plan to do just that. Knowing that Tamar was a great cook, he pretended to be ill and requested that she come to his room and bring him food. Once in the room, he violated her. Tamar tried to resist Amnon's advances, but he overpowered her. After committing his sinful act, Amnon's love turned to hate. He became disgusted with Tamar and insisted that she leave his room. Not knowing what to do, she fled to her brother Absalom.

Upon hearing of this incident, Tamar's father, King David, seems to have been bewildered. He neglected to punish or hold accountable his son Amnon for his unacceptable behavior. Why? We do not know. Perhaps it was because he thought about his own sinful actions with Bathsheba and associated it with the retribution of God. We do know, however, that Absalom hated

Amnon for raping his sister. This incident simmered in Absalom's heart for two years, until he

Was able to arranged the murder of his half-brother for having violated Tamar. After Amnon was killed, Absalom had to flee his father's house in order to avoid David's wrath. He took refuge with Talmai, son of Ammihud, King of Geshur, for three years. Talmai was Absalom's maternal grandfather (2 Samuel 13:37–38; 1 Chronicles 3:1–3).

When polygamy is practiced in the home and boundaries are not defined and strict discipline is not maintained, it can be a temptation for incest to creep in among the siblings through future generations.

# ZERUIAH

*2 Samuel 17:25*
*1 Chronicles 1–16*

Zeruiah is one of King David's two sisters who are mentioned in Scripture. The other is Abigal, the mother of Amasa, Absalom's military general.

Zeruiah had three sons: Joab, Asahel, and Abishai. These sons were very well-known in the kingdom, as they were all mighty men of war. (Joab was David's military leader.) They were also King David's first cousins. They were sometimes ruthless and hard to deal with. Asahel's eagerness to show off brought him to an untimely death after he insisted on dueling with the mighty Abner, Saul's military leader. Years later, Joab, against David's wishes, avenged his brother's death by killing Abner. This caused David great distress and sorrow. Joab was also responsible for the death of Absalom, King David's son, even though David had specifically instructed Joab not to hurt Absalom. Joab did many, many other things against King David's wishes. Joab, Asahel, and Abishai were the perpetrators of many horrendous and heinous acts that displeased King David. Joab was vindictive, unmerciful, and ruthless; he feared neither God nor man. These brothers were "a force to be reckoned with." On one occasion, David stated, "These sons of Zeruiah be too hard for me" (2 Samuel 3:39). Although David appreciated their abilities, he hated their attitudes.

When David was on his deathbed and issuing final instructions to his son Solomon, he included the command, "Do not let Joab's hoary head go down in peace." Solomon had Joab executed, although Joab had pleaded for mercy on the horns of the altar.

The fact that Zeruiah's name appears twenty-five times in the Bible along with her sons' names, and never the father's name, indicates that she was a mother of distinction who had a strong influence on her sons. Their quick tempers were, perhaps, inherited from her, which paints a negative picture of her. Although she had a profound influence, it was not a positive one, I'm afraid.

# DAVID'S SIX WIVES IN HEBRON

*1 Samuel 3:2–5*
*2 Samuel 5:1–5*
*1 Chronicles 3:1–3*

David reigned in Hebron for seven years and in Jerusalem for thirty- three years and six months. He was about seventy-one years old when he died.

| David's Wife | Son/Daughter | Remarks |
| --- | --- | --- |
| Ahinoam | Amnon | Raped his half-sister Tamar; killed by his brother Absalom |
| Abigail | Chileab(Daniel) | See the chapter titled "Abigail (David's Wife)" |
| Maacah | Absalom and Tamar | Daughter of Talmai, King of Geshur |
| | | When Absalom was fleeing from David, he went to his grandfather's house (2 Samuel 13:37–38) |

| David's Wife | Son/Daughter | Remarks |
|---|---|---|
| Haggith | Adonijah | Attempted to be king twice; executed by his brother Solomon |
| Abital | Shephatiah | Scripture is silent. |
| Eglah | Ithream | Scripture is silent. |

# RIZPAH

*2 Sam 3:7; 21:1-14*

Rizpah was one of King Saul's concubines. She and King Saul had two sons: Armoni and Mephibosheth. Her father's name was Aiah. After Saul's death, David became king. Thereafter came a three-year famine in the land. King David asked the Lord the reason for the famine. God told him it was because King Saul had dishonored an oath that Joshua had made with the Gibeonites (although Joshua had made the agreement based on inaccurate information the Gibeonites had deliberately given him). But because Joshua had sworn by the name of God, God held Himself accountable for the oath. Over the years, this agreement had been carefully upheld. The oath that Joshua had taken in the Lord's name was broken when King Saul declared war against the Gibeonites.

The Gibeonites requested that an atonement be made for King Saul's breach. As a result, seven of Saul's sons were to be hanged in Gibeah. Now I know this is a strange requirement—a harsh one, to say the least—to be supported by the God of love. Remember, however, that God couldn't break His law. He Himself atoned for our sins by offering His own Son as a sacrifice.

So King David took the five sons of Merab and Adriel, who had been brought up by Michal (Merab's sister and King David's wife), and Armoni and Mephibosheth, the sons of Rizpah, and executed them in the sight of the people. What a terrible day. He hanged them on seven gallows on a hill on the first day of the barley harvest.

After her sons were dead, Rizpah, wearing sackcloth, appeared at the site. She spread sackcloth on the rocks underneath the gallows upon which her sons had been slain. This grief-stricken mother kept watch for five months. She drove away the vultures and all wild beasts. She stayed from the time of the barley harvest until the season of rain. Night and day, she guarded her dead, keeping away wild animals and vultures.. In the heat of day and in the cold of night, she faithfully stayed her course, never relinquishing.

When King David heard of this mother's long vigil for her dead sons, he commanded the seven bodies to be taken down and buried with those of Saul and Jonathan. Rizpah's mission was accomplished; her devotion had prevailed.

The death of these seven individuals, and the sorrow and the grief of this mother, were the consequences of King Saul's sinful act, an act in which neither Rizpah nor her sons had played a part.

I am reminded of another mother in the New Testament who stood by and watched her son suffer and die for sins in which He had no part. Because of His love, Jesus Christ hung on the cross, suffered, and gave His life to atone for sins He did not commit. He died for your sins and mine.

Rizpah's love and persistence were rewarded. "Be not weary in well doing for in due time you shall reap, if you faint not" (Galatians 6:9).

# ABIGAIL (DAVID'S SISTER)

*2 Samuel 17:25*
*1 Chronicles 2:16, 17*

Abigail is one of David's two sisters mentioned in Scripture. The other is Zeruiah. Abigail and Zeruiah's father's name was Nahash, not Jesse. Some scholars speculate that their mother had been married earlier to someone else.

Abigail was the mother of Amasa, Absalom's general during the time when Absalom attempted to overthrow his father, David's throne. Previous to that, Amasa was one of King David's mighty men. David was Amasa's uncle. Unlike his cousins Joab, Asahel, and Abishai, Amasa appears to have been more like a gentle giant.

Amasa's life came to an abrupt end, without warning, when his first cousin Joab, Zeruiah's son, killed him.

Abigail was the wife of Jether, who is also referred to as Ithra in some places in the Bible. Her name is not mentioned as much as her sister's name, Zeruiah. Abigail possessed a meek and quiet spirit, as did her son Amasa. Undoubtedly, her influence had a lot to do with Amasa's calm temperament.

# BATHSHEBA

*1 Samuel 11:15*
*1 Chronicles 3:1–9*

Bathsheba's father's name was Eliam, sometimes called Ammiel, meaning "God is gracious." I think it is safe to assume that Bathsheba's family was God-fearing. Her father as well as her husband, Uriah, were gallant soldiers in King David's army.

Bathsheba's story is but a chapter in the story of King David—and a most bittersweet chapter at that. Her story is perhaps the only well-known story in the Bible in which the leading lady says very few words. This is her story in a nutshell:

It was the time of year when kings went to war. David, however, stayed home. He took a walk on his rooftop. He saw a young woman taking a bath. Finding her to be beautiful, he sent for her. She was the wife of Uriah the Hittite.

David lay with Bathsheba in his bedchamber. She became pregnant. Later, she sent him a note that read, "I am with child."

David started scheming to cover up the facts in order to save himself, but his scheme didn't work. After that, he had Uriah placed on the front line of battle to be killed. Uriah was, indeed, killed.

After Bathsheba's seven days of mourning for her husband, David sent for her. She became his wife. David thought he was safe, but God had seen everything he had done.

God sent the prophet Nathan to expose David. Nathan told David an allegory about a man who had one little ewe; another man who had many ewes took the first man's one ewe. This story angered David, and before seeing himself in the allegory, he passed judgment on villiam who was himself. After Nathan told him that he was the man, he repented, crying bitter tears. Nathan told David that he had been forgiven, but he said that Bathsheba's baby would not live. David lay on the ground, praying and fasting, during the baby's illness. After seven days passed, the baby died. David rose up, washed himself, and resumed his responsibilities.

Bathsheba and David had four more sons: Solomon, Shobab, Jonathan, and Shemei. (1 Chron.3:6.) Scripture is silent in reference to their characters and acomplishments.

Many years later when David was on his deathbed, Adonijah, his eldest living son, attempted to take the kingdom and become king. However, the throne had already been promised to Solomon.

When Adonijah's plan was crushed, he went to Bathsheba and requested that she ask Solomon for Abishag, David's last concubine, the one who had cared for David in his last days. Solomon became furious at Bathsheba and Adonijah. He had Adonijah executed.

I don't know if Bathsheba was naive or unlearned in the ways of protocol concerning a deceased king. According to the law, this marriage between Adonijah and Abishag would give Adonijah an advantage over Solomon.

There is nothing in this story showing that Bathsheba felt sorry or repented of this adulterous act. David? Yes, he did feel remorse. It is believed that Bathsheba did repent and become a good mother.

It appears that she was David's favorite wife. Scripture is silent about her three other sons. It is evident that she maintained her influence over David until the end, because she reminded him of his promise to make Solomon his successor instead of any of his other sons. Perhaps Bathsheba used her mistake as a lesson and became a better person, accepting God's forgiveness and becoming a person of integrity. Her son, Solomon, is credited with penning the words, "Train up a child in the way he should go and when he is old he will not depart" (Proverbs 22:6).

The Scripture says of King David, "David did what was right in the eyes of the Lord, and had not turned aside from anything that He commanded him all the days of his life, *except in the matter of Uriah, the Hittite*" (1 Kings 15:5, emphasis added).

What a great commendation!

Tradition says that it was Bathsheba who composed Proverbs 31 as an admonition to Solomon upon his marriage to Pharaoh's daughter.

# ABISHAG

*1 Kings 1:3, 4; 2:13–25*

When King David was old and feeble, lying on his deathbed (at the age of seventy), his body could not be warmed. So his servants, who were perhaps medical advisors, recommended that a fresh young maiden be found to cherish him, meaning to nurse him and to be his concubine. I submit that this was an acceptable practice during biblical times, but it was not something condoned by God. The idea behind bringing a concubine to David was that this would give the king the advantage of the woman's superabundant vitality.

Abishag, a beautiful, young Shunammite woman, was chosen for the task. Very lovely, she cared for the king and served him, but he did not know her, meaning that the two did not have sexual contact.

After King David's death, Adonijah, David's oldest living son, who was Solomon's half-brother (at this point, Adonijah had already attempted to usurp the throne once), went to Bathsheba to ask her to influence Solomon and lead him to grant Adonijah Abishag's hand in marriage. Solomon construed Adonijah's request as virtual treason, seeing that a man who married a deceased king's wife inherited the late king's legal rights. With his keen insight, Solomon saw what was behind Adonijah's wish to marry Abishag. Solomon ordered Benaiah, who was once one of

David's mighty men but now one of Solomon's mighty men to slay Adonijah.

Innocent Abishag caused quite a stir just by being herself.

# DELILAH

*Judges 16:4-20*

Delilah was a Philistine woman from the valley of Sorek, which extended from a place near Jerusalem to the Mediterranean Sea. She was the heartless wrecker of the mighty man Samson, the twelfth judge of Israel who judged for twenty years.

It is impossible to tell Delilah's story without mentioning her relationship with Samson.

It is said of Samson that he was physically strong but morally weak. He could rend a lion, but he could not overcome his lust. He could break his bonds, but not his negative habits. He could conquer Philistines, but not his passions.

Herbert Lockyer states, "Delilah was a woman of unholy persistence and devilish deceit, who had a personal charm, mental ability, self-command, and nerve, but who used all her qualities for one purpose: money. She and womanly honor and love had never met, for behind her beautiful face was a heart as dark as hell, and full of viperous treachery." The lords of the Philistines offered Delilah eleven hundred pieces of silver to learn and tell them the secret of Samson's strength.

Considering that Judas sold out Jesus for only thirty pieces of silver, we see that this was a large sum of money and a great temptation to Delilah. Using her seductive skills, she tried three times, to no avail, to get Samson to reveal the secret of his strength. Jokingly, he gave her three different answers. The first time, he said to tie him up with green twigs; the second time, to tie him with a new rope; the third time, to braid his hair. Each time Delilah spoke with Samson about his strength, the Philistine lords were secretly hidden nearby, ready to pounce upon him, but Samson escaped. Then Delilah tried her last strategy. She sighed, whined, and, perhaps, leaned on Samson's chest, talking in a submissive voice. She said, "How can you say 'you love me,' when your heart is not with me? You have mocked me these three times, and have not told me where your great strength lies." She pestered him daily with her words and pressed him (all the while, thinking about the money) until his soul was vexed. The pestering became unbearable.

Samson finally relented and told Delilah the secret of his supernatural strength. He said, "No razor has ever come upon my head, for I have been a Nazarite to God from my mother's womb. If I am shaven, then my strength will leave me, and I shall become weak, and be like any other man." Immediately, Delilah sent for the lords of the Philistines. She lulled Samson to sleep on her knees, and then the lords cut off the locks of his hair. When Samson awakened, he found that his strength was gone. The lords captured and imprisoned him. Delilah received her eleven hundred pieces of silver in blood money and then went on her way, looking for her next victim. That is the end of her story as we know it.

After the lords captured Samson and put him in prison, they gouged out his eyes. Out of the depths of his heart, Samson cried unto the Lord. The Lord heard his soulful petition. Samson knew that his pathetic predicament was caused by his disobedience to the Lord God of heaven. His hair began to grow. God restored unto this once sinful, but now repentant, servant the strength he had lost.

The Philistines called a great celebration to offer sacrifice to their god Dagon. When their hearts were merry, they called for the pathetic creature, Samson to perform for them. Then Samson's extreme circumstances became God's opportunity. Samson threw his arms around the pillars of the magnificent temple, causing it to tumble down. The three thousand Philistines, including the evil Delilah (we believe), perished. It was a victory that cost Samson his own life. Scripture says that he killed more in his death than he had killed in his life.

What Samson did not accomplish spiritually during times of peace, he had to accomplished during the time of his troubles.

For the lips of an immoral woman drip honey, and her mouth is smoother than oil; but in the end she is bitter as wormwood, sharp as a two-edged sword. Her feet go down to death, her steps lay hold of hell. Lest you ponder her path of life—her ways are unstable; you do not know them. Therefore hear me now, my children, and do not depart from the words of my mouth. Remove your way far from her, and do not go near the door of her house. (Proverbs 5:3–8)

# NAAMAH

*1 Kings 14:21, 31*
*2 Chronicles 12–13*


Of Solomon's three hundred wives, Naamah was the first lady, or number one among the wives. Naamah was from the royal line of the Ammonite nation (the descendants of Lot; see Genesis 19:36– 38), one of Israel's great nemesis. The Ammonites were heathens. Their god was Moloch. Since Naamah was the leading lady, she received many favors from her husband, Solomon. One favor was the erecting of a high place for her god, Moloch. Naamah's influence on the king was offensive to the people of Israel, as they witnessed her leading Solomon deeper and deeper into idolatry. She was the mother of Solomon's successor, Rehoboam. Evidently, Rehoboam was also greatly influenced by her. The last note we see about his life mentions that his ways displeased the Lord.

Rehoboam was the last king of the United Monarchy of Israel. It was because of his immature and irrational decision making that the kingdom was split. Two tribes remained with him, those of Benjamin and Judah. The other ten tribes went with Jeroboam, who was previously Solomon's right-hand man. These latter tribes are generally referred to as the lost tribes or the northern tribes. They eventually established their capital in Samaria and eventually became known as the Samaritans.

Through one of His servants, the prophet Ahijah, God had given this prophecy about the tribes years before they split. It was not predestined, however.

, just foreknowledge. God knows all things, as He reads the hearts of men and women. So He knew the characters of Jeroboam and Rehoboam before they were born—and the character of the latter's mother as well. The same can be said for each of us.

# ZERUAH

*1 Kings 11:26–40*


Zeruah is always referred to in Scripture as the widow of Nebat, an Ephraimite from Zeredah. Their son was Jeroboam, who led the ten tribes of Israel into idolatry. Jeroboam served under King Solomon until the prophet Ahijah related to him the prophecy that one day he would rule over 10 of the 12 tribes of Israel. This angered Solomon, so he threatened Jeroboam. Jeroboam had to flee for his life. So he fled to Egypt. He returned after Solomon died, then he rebelled against Solomon's son Rehoboam. This split the Kingdom just as Ahijah had prophised.

Occasionally, Jeroboam's name is written as "Jeroboam, the son of Nebat." This is an indication that his character was more aligned with his father's than with his mother's. This indicates that his mother was not the one who influenced him in making the evil decision to separate the kingdom. God had told Jeroboam through the prophet Ahijah that the kingdom would be divided because some of the tribes had forsaken God and had begun to worship other gods. Jeroboam was to be the one to lead the ten tribes. If he had exercised a little faith and patience, then God would have reigned over the kingdom in His own way. Instead, God left two of the tribes (Judah and Benjamin) with Rehoboam, giving Jeroboam the tribes of Reuben, Simeon, Levi, Zebulun, Issachar, Dan, Asher, Naphtali, Manassah, and Ephraim. Afterward, the people of those ten tribes went deeper into idolatry—and their end was worse than their beginning.

Whether Zeruah was an idol worshipper or not, we do not know. But we can safely assume that she was not the major influence in her son's irrational actions.

# JERUSHAH

*2 Kings 15:33*
*1 Chronicles 6:12*
*2 Chronicles 27:1–6*

Jerushah's father was Zadok, a priest who served during the reign of King David. She married godly King Uzziah, who had become king at the age of sixteen and who ruled for fifty-two years. Uzziah died a leper because of his attempt to burn incense in the temple, an act that was solely the responsibility of the priest.

To the union of Jerushah and Uzziah was born a son. Jotham was his name. Jotham served his nation as a regent while his father lived. After his father's death, he became king and ruled for sixteen years.

Although Jotham's father made one fatal mistake and was removed from the temple and was placed in a home for lepers for eleven years until he died, Jotham's home was, evidently, a godly home. The Scripture reads, "He did that which was right in the sight of the Lord." Jotham became mighty because he prepared his ways before the Lord. What an honor to his parents.

# NAOMI, RUTH, AND ORPAH

*Ruth 1–4*

In the days when judges ruled and there was a famine in the land, a certain man, Elimelech of Bethlehem, Judea, went to dwell in the country of Moab. He took with him his wife, Naomi, and their two sons, Mahlon and Kilion.

In the course of time, Elimelech died. One of his sons married Ruth, and his other son married Orpah. Both young women were Moabites. Eventually, Mahlon and Kilion died. The Scriptures are silent about the cause of their deaths. Neither couple had had any children. At that time, it had been ten years since Naomi had first arrived in Moab. In the land of Moab, she heard that the Lord had visited His people in Bethlehem, Judea, and had given them bread. The famine was over. So Naomi determined to return to Bethlehem.

When she informed her daughters-in-law, they were determined to go with her. She explained her situation and said that she was returning to nothing. She encouraged them to return to their families, but they refused.

As the women traveled to Bethlehem, Orpah's mind began to wander. She wondered if she had done the right thing by following Naomi. Just as Lot's wife looked back and was destroyed, Orpah looked back. Moab was very much in her heart. She kissed her aged mother-in-law, said good-bye, and returned to her own people and to her own god. Back to Moab and Moloch she went, simultaneously sending herself into obscurity. At that point, she vanishes from the pages of sacred history.

Ruth clung to her mother-in-law and begged her not to leave her. From this relationship sprang the most beautiful quotation about love in all the world.

"Entreat me not to leave you, or to turn back from following after you; for wherever you go, I will go; and wherever you lodge, I will lodge. Your people shall be my people, and your God, my God. Where you die, I will die, and there will I be buried. The Lord do so to me and more also, if anything but death parts you and me." Ruth 1:16-17.

Upon entering the city, Naomi saw that there was great excitement in her old community. The word of her arrival passed from mouth to mouth, from house to house. Many came out to see Naomi. But some asked, "Is this Naomi?" The woman whose very name meant "beautiful and pleasant" had changed. Ten years in Moab, with all its anguish and grief, hardship and the loss of fellowship with God and His people, had dried up Naomi's happy feelings. She could not bear the contradiction between the name she bore and the person she was. She said, "Call me not Naomi, but call me Mara (bitter) for the Almighty hath dealt very bitterly with me. I went out full and the Lord hath brought me home again empty; I have returned, husbandless, childless and penniless."

Naomi and Ruth, clinging to each other, plunged into poverty and despair. Under Jewish law at the time, the poor were allowed to harvest from any field. Ruth was qualified, physical and economical, for performing the humble task of following the reapers and gathering up their gleanings for her aged mother-in-law, Naomi, and for herself. So Ruth went out and secured work as a gleaner in the fields, by the providence of God, in the field of Boaz.

Ruth was not aware of how exceptionally the Lord would reward her devotion to her mother-in-law. Ruth's beauty and industry attracted Boaz's attention. He inquired as to her identity. He was told by his servant that she was the Moabitess who had come with Naomi from her own land. Because of Ruth's diligence, Boaz instructed his servant to leave a little more of the harvest for her. When she came home with more than she should actually have, Naomi inquired why. After being told whose field Ruth was gleaning, Naomi understood. Boaz was a godly man, a man of intelligence with a high code of morals. He was also kin to Naomi. He appreciated Ruth's quiet loveliness, her purity, and her industrious ways. So he began to shower her with small favors.

Naomi was knowledgeable of the law regarding the rights and responsibilities of a kinsperson as pertaining to a deceased relative. She not only knew the law, but was also wise in the ways of men toward women. She sensed that Boaz was attracted to Ruth and that Ruth felt a softness for him. The scene was now set for a beautiful romance. Naomi took her next step because she wanted a brighter future for her beloved daughter-in-law. She directed Ruth to put on her best clothing and to go to the threshing floor at night. Ruth trusted and respected the wisdom of her mother-in-law. Naomi further instructed Ruth to lie at Boaz's feet and to uncover his feet while he slept. Boaz discovered Ruth in the night and asked why she was there. She explained to him that Naomi's land needed a redeemer. The godly Boaz listened intently and promised that he would look into the matter. He knew there was a man whose kinship to Naomi was closer than his own. Boaz decided to check with that man first. If that man would not redeem Naomi's land, then Boaz would. After settling these matters in his mind, Boaz counseled Ruth to leave before dawn so as to safeguard her reputation.

The measure recommended by Naomi and adopted by Ruth was a legal calling on Boaz, as the supposed nearest kinsman of the family, to fulfilled the duty required of that relationship. He immediately sent word to Naomi that he gladly accepted the legal responsibility of protecting her and her daughter-in-law.

In biblical times, the nearest kinsman was sometimes referred to as a GOEL. A GOEL was a relative whose job it was to come to the rescue of kin. This position was codified in the law specific to a levirate, which is spoken of in Deuteronomy 25. It includes the idea of redemption or deliverance, with the goel being a "kinsman-redeemer." The GOEL was usually a well-established male in the extended family whose responsibility was to protect the family's honor. The GOEL could buy back family lands that had been sold in times of hardship (Leviticus 25:23–28) and could pay the redemption price for family members who had been sold into slavery (Leviticus 25:47–49). And in this case, if the GOEL was single or otherwise free to marry, he could perpetuate the family line when a family member died without an heir. The GOEL did this by marrying the widow and then fathering offspring who would go on to inherit the name and property of the one who had died. There was a redemptive aspect to the GOEL'S function. Every kinsman- redeemer was a living illustration of the position and work of Christ in relationship to His redeemed. He is our true kinsman-Redeemer who became our brother, who redeems us from our bondage to Satan, who redeems our lives from death, and who returns us to a right standing with Him. This is justification.

The day after Ruth came to him at night, Boaz located the next of kin. The man waived his right to redeem the land.

Boaz had proven his honorable and businesslike character by going to the gates of the city of Bethlehem and appearing before the elders. Then he went forth publicly to tell the elders that he had bought Ruth the Moabitess, Naomi's daughter-in-law, to be his wife. The beautiful, industrious, and humble Ruth became the wife of a rich and honorable man who was known in the city. By her faithfulness, she achieved the seemingly impossible: she was lifted out of poverty and came to enjoy influence and a life of plenty. This marriage of Ruth and Boaz ensured the Moabite woman who had previously worshipped Moloch a place in the lineage of our Lord and Savior, Jesus the Christ.

After Ruth and Boaz's son Obed was born, Naomi's neighbors, rejoicing with her, said, "Thy daughter-in-law, which loveth thee, which is better to thee than seven sons, hath born him." Naomi, looking through tears, joyfully took over the duties of nursing her grandchild.

Naomi could surely say, "Weeping may endure for a night, but joy cometh in the morning" (Psalm 30:5).

As it is of some of the other women mentioned in this book, the following is true of Ruth: "Who can find a virtuous wife? For her worth is far above rubies. … Her husband is known in the city gates when he sits among the elders of the land. … Give her of the fruit of her hands and let her own works praise her in the gates" (Proverbs 31:10, 23, 31).

# JEZEBEL

*1 Kings 16:32; 18; 19; 21*
*2 Kings 9:7*

Jezebel was the daughter of Ethball, who was king of the Zidonians in Tyre. She was the wife of King Ahab of Israel; the mother of Jehoram, King of Israel; the mother-in-law of Joram, King of Judah; and the grandmother of Ahaziah, King of Judah. Jezebel and Ahab's marriage formed part of an alliance that King Omri of Israel had made with the Phoenicians. The alliance was sealed by the marriage of the King of Tyre's daughter, the strong-willed, mean hearted, domineering Princess Jezebel, to Omri's son and heir, Prince Ahab, a marriage that produced one of the most notoriously immoral and dramatic stories in the Bible. I think the term for the union nowadays would be "a marriage made in hell." The part Jezebel played in her husband's nineteen-year reign was such that her name, even today, is a synonym for a shameless, immoral woman.

As a child, Jezebel was a worshiper of Baal. She continued to worship Baal during her reign as queen and tried to influence the people of Israel to do likewise. A great battle ensued between Jehovah and Baal; the visible participants were God's prophet,Elijah and Queen Jezebel and her prophets.

To please his wife, Ahab built an altar to Baal in Samaria. Jezebel commanded 450 prophets of Baal. She slew all the prophets of

Jehovah that she could find. Obadiah took a hundred prophets of Jehovah and hid them fifty to a cave, feeding them with bread and water. But the prophet Elijah was a thorn in Jezebel's side. She really wanted to get her hands on him. When she heard of the results of the showdown at Mount Carmel between the prophet Elijah and her own Baal-worshipping prophets, Jezebel became doubly furious and threatened Elijah's life.

She took Naboth's vineyard for Ahab after having its owner executed. When the prophet Elijah heard of this, he prophesied to Ahab that God's vengeance would fall upon him. In the same place where Naboth died, the dogs would lick Ahab's blood; the house of Ahab would be completely destroyed; and the dogs would eat his wife, Jezebel. Sure enough, Ahab was killed in battle, and the dogs did lick his blood. Jezebel continued to have an evil influence on Israel for about ten years after Ahab's death.

The prophet,Elijah, by God's instruction, anointed Jehu king and commanded him to avenge the blood of the prophets and servants of Jehovah. And that Jehu did.

Jezebel stood by the window, her face painted and her body dressed in full queenly attire. As Jehu entered the gates to the castle in his chariot, she shouted down to him from her window, "Had Zimri peace, who slew his master?" (Zimri was another chariot captain who had revolted against his king and set fire to the palace at Tirzah. He died in the wreckage.) Jehu focused his eyes on Jezebel, who was standing in the palace window on the second floor. Jehu yelled to the queen's attendants, asking them to throw her down. They did so gladly. Jehu drove over Jezebel's body with his chariot. He later gave instructions for her to be buried. But it was later discovered that dogs had eaten everything except her skull, feet, and hands. She was not honored by being buried in a tomb. The dogs had eaten the flesh of this evil woman who had attempted to rule without God, but by her own selfish power. The prophecy had been fulfilled.

Jezebel is a prime example of everything a woman ought not to be. It is a common saying that, "A heartless woman is more dangerous than a heartless man. A God-fearing woman does often excel men in goodness. The Godly woman can bless lives more than man can ever attempt to do." But the latter was not the case for Jezebel. The former was definitely the case for Jezebel, for that she was: a heartless woman.

# ATHALIAH

*2 Kings 8:26; 11:11, 2, 3, 13, 14, 20*
*2 Chronicles 22:2, 10, 11, 12; 23:12, 13, 21; 24:7*

Athaliah was the granddaughter of Omri, the sixth king of Israel. The daughter of Omri's evil son Ahab and Ahab's wicked wife, Jezebel, Athaliah was the only queen/woman to reign in the kingdom of Judah. Athaliah was married to Jehoram, the king of the southern kingdom of Judah who was the son of Good King Jehoshaphat. Athaliah was from the northern kingdom (*Israel*).

Samaria was the capital of the northern kingdom of Israel. Jerusalem was the capital of the southern kingdom of Judah.

When Jehoram arrived in Jerusalem with his new bride, Athaliah, she immediately went about to fill Jerusalem with the doctrine of Baal worship. Not only was she zealous in spreading the doctrine of Baal, but she was also determined to wipe out all knowledge and worship of the true God, Jehovah.

Because his brothers were loyal to the faith of their nation, King Jehoram slew all of them with the sword. He also killed the princes of Israel (2 Chronicles 21:6).

Elijah the prophet prophesied the death of Jehoram.

> Thus saith the Lord God of David thy father, because thou hast not walked in the ways of

> Jehoshaphat thy father, nor in the way of Asa,
> King of Judah, but hast walked in the way of
> the kings of Israel, and hast made Judah and
> the inhabitants of Jerusalem to go a whoring,
> like to the whoredoms of the house of Ahab,
> and also hast slain thy brethren of thy father's
> house, which were better than thyself Behold,
> the Lord will strike your people with a serious
> affliction-your children, your wives, and all your
> possessions.......After all this the Lord struck him
> in his intestines with an incurable disease...... so
> he died in severe pain. (2 Chronicles 21:12–18)

After reigning for eight years, Jehoram died of an incurable disease. While he reigned, he was greatly influenced by Athaliah, who possessed a domineering spirit like her mother, Jezebel. The couple's son Ahaziah reigned in Jehoram's stead. The Scriptures tell us that Ahaziah "walked in the ways of the house of Ahab, for his mother was his counselor to do wickedly" (2 Chronicles 22:3).

After reigning for one year, Ahaziah was slain by Jehu, who had been anointed by the Lord to cut off the house of Ahab. After Athaliah heard that her son was dead, she had all the heirs of the house of Judah massacred, or so she thought. Athaliah's selfish ambition caused her to murder her own grandchildren.

Fortunately for the kingdom of Judah, Jehosheba, Athaliah's stepdaughter and Joash's aunt, rescued Joash from the bloody massacre which occurred when Athaliah came to the throne. Jehosheba hid the child for six years while the evil Queen Athaliah reigned. At the appropriate time, Jehosheba's husband, High Priest

Jehoida, brought forth the child, who was now seven years old and crowned him as king, with the aid of some of the mighty men of battle. When Athaliah heard the noise of the people celebrating the young king's ascension to the throne, she cried, "Treason! Treason!" Jehoiada, the priest, ordered that she be slain outside the temple. She was slain as she entered the horses' gate by the palace, close to the temple. The horses then trampled over her body where it lay dead at the gates. Like her evil mother in life and in death, Athaliah died without pity. Athaliah, was selfish— only what she wanted mattered to her. And those who hindered her mission must be destroyed.

We reap what we sow. Jesus said, "For all they that take the sword shall perish with the sword" (Matthew 26:52).

# JEHOSHEBA

*2 Kings 11:2*
*2 Chronicles 22:11*

The name Jehosheba means "Jehovah is her oath"; Jehosheba's name refers to a solemn promise of God.

Jehosheba was the daughter of King Jehoram by another wife, not Athaliah, and was the half sister of the slain King Ahaziah. She was married to the high priest Jehoiada. Hers is the only biblical situation known of a princess marrying a high priest.

When wicked Queen Athaliah massacred most of the royal family's males (heirs to the throne), Jehosheba hid the only survivor in the temple. The survivor was King Ahaziah's son, Jehosheba's nephew, Joash. She hid him for six years, until he was seven years old, which was the minimum age for one to be crowned as king. (In other words, Hebrew custom dictated that no king could be younger than seven years of age.) The boy's grandmother Queen Athaliah was then dethroned and destroyed. She was executed.

Jehosheba was a courageous woman. She preserved the Messianic line. To her goes the credit of preserving the "seed royale." If Joash had been destroyed, then the line of Judah would have become extinct and Baal worship would have become supreme. God's promise to King David was, "If your sons take heed to their ways, to walk before Me in truth with all their hearts and with all their soul … you shall not lack a man on the throne of Israel" (1 Kings 2:4). "And He who promised is faithful" (Hebrews 10:23).

Jehosheba and her husband became the instruments through whom God worked to save King David's kingdom and preserve the royal lineage through which Jesus the Christ is descended.

# JEHOADDIN

*2 Kings 14:2*
*2 Chronicles 24:3; 25:1*

Jehoaddin was a stepdaughter of Athaliah. She became the wife of Joash. Joash had been rescued from the infamous massacre by being hidden by Jehosheba and her husband, Jehoiada the high priest, until he was seven years old. He was then brought forth and crowned as king. Athaliah was dethroned. Joash reigned for twenty-seven years. Jehoaddin gave birth to a son, whom she named Amaziah. After Jehoaddin's husband, Joash, became ill and was slain in bed, Amaziah. succeeded his slain father. Joash began a righteous rule that later deteriorated. He introduced idolatry into his kingdom. Remember, he was married to Athaliah's stepdaughter. A little negative influence goes a long way.

# ABI, OR ABIJAH

*2 Kings 18:2*
*2 Chronicles 29:1; 26:5*

Abi was the daughter of Zachariah, who is believed to be Zachariah the minor prophet. Abi was married to the godless King Ahaz of Israel.

Abi's most important, notable accomplishment in her life was that she was the mother of the godly King Hezekiah. Because of her staunch faith in Jehovah God, she was able to counteract the evil influence of her ungodly husband, King Ahaz, on her son Hezekiah. Led by God, about whom his mother had taught him, Hezekiah was able to bring about a mighty religious revival. The Scripture says of him, "He did that which was right in the sight of the Lord according to all that King David, his ancestor had done."

Today, there are many mothers like Abi who have godless husbands but who, because of their own influence, have good Christian children.

# JECHOLIAH

*2 Kings 22:1*
*2 Chronicles 26:3*

Jecholiah was the wife of King Amaziah, the ninth king of Judah. She was the mother of King Uzziah, or Azariah, as he is sometimes referred to. Not much is known about Jecholiah, but one statement does get our attention: "Her son, King Uzziah, did that which was right in the sight of God, and that he prospered so long as he sought the Lord." This is strong evidence of Jecholiah's good influence on her child.

Although he stepped outside of God's grace as an old man, his good deeds will always be remembered.

# JEDIDAH

*2 Kings 22:1, 2*

Jedidah was the wife of wicked King Amon and the mother of good King Josiah. What a contrast! King Amon was murdered in his bed by his own servants. Josiah succeeded his slain father, King Amon, when he was only eight years old. He reigned successfully for thirty-one years. The Scripture says that he did that which was right and pleasing in God's sight all the days of his life.

Upon remodeling the temple and the finding of the "Book of the Law", which is believed to have been the book of Deuteronomy, he called in Huldah, the prophetess. After consulting with Huldah the prophetess, Josiah instituted a revival to bring the people back to the worship of the true God, according to what was written in the law.

Although Josiah had a wicked father, Jedidah, his mother must have been a godly woman who greatly influenced her son, for after his name appears in the Bible, we read these words: "And he did that which was right in the sight of the Lord."

# HULDAH

*2 Kings 22:14–20*
*2 Chronicles 34:22–28*

Huldah, a prophetess during the reign of Josiah, King of Judah, was wife of Shallum, who was keeper of the king's wardrobe and who dwelt in the second quarter of Jerusalem.

Josiah was eight years old when he became king. He reigned for thirty-one years in Jerusalem. He did what was right in the sight of the Lord, walking in the ways of his forefather David. He did not turn aside to the right hand or to the left.

It was during Josiah's reign that, after he had ordered the repair of the temple, Hilkiah, the high priest, found in the temple the book of the Lord given by Moses. Hilkiah immediately took the book to King Josiah, who sent for Huldah the prophetess to determine the authenticity of the book. Being a true prophet, Huldah immediately recognized it and identified it as the real thing. Then she gave a prophecy (a message from God). She prophesied that the nation would fall to ruin because its people disobeyed the commands of God. Her message was accepted as one from God Himself, and it greatly influenced the many reforms that followed, which were implemented by King Josiah.

The fact that the king sent for Huldah the prophetess to authenticate the writings when there were many male prophets in Judah at that time,(even Jeremiah), speaks very highly of Huldah's reputation and credibility.

# HAMUTAL

*2 Kings 23:31; 24:18*
*Jeremiah 13:18; 52:1*
*Ezekiel 19*

Hamutal was the wife of Good King Josiah of Judah and the daughter of Jeremiah of Libnah. She was also the mother of two of Judah's last kings. King Jehoahaz, who succeeded his father, Josiah. During Jehoahaz's reign of only three months, he displeased the Lord. He was taken prisoner by Pharaoh Neco of Egypt. Mattaniah, whose name was changed to Zedekiah by Pharaoh Neco, ruled eleven years and also displeased the Lord. He was the last king of Judah. He was taken captive by Nebuchadnezzar. His sons were killed before his eyes and his own eyes were put out. He was taken to Babylon; and there he died.

There were two kings between Jehoahaz and Zedekiah, Jehoiakim and Jehoiachin. These were Josiah's son and Josiah's grandson, respectively, but they were not Hamutal's blood relations.

Hamutal was married to the last good king of Judah. Her two sons who succeeded him were bad boys. Whenever the phrase, "his mother's name was", occurs, this indicate that the personality of the child, whether good or bad, is more aligned with the mother. Jeremiah's joint message to the king and the queen mother in Jeremiah 13:18 seems to indicate that they both had earned their judgment.

The twenty-third chapter of Ezekiel is an allegory about two sisters. It depicts the condition of Judah and Israel and their people's relationship to God. I suggest you read it.

# MAACAH, OR MAACHAH

*2 Chronicles 11:20-22*
*1 Kings 15:10-13*

Maacah was the granddaughter of King David's son Absalom and the favorite wife of King Rehoboam, Absalom's nephew. She was named after her great-grandmother Maacah, who was one of King David's six wives when he lived in Hebron for seven years. Grandmother Maacah was the mother of Absalom and Tamar. Rehoboam was the first king of Judah. Before Rehoboam, there was no separation between the kingdom of Israel and the kingdom of Judah. It was all one kingdom.

Rehoboam had eighteen wives and sixty concubines. Maacah was his favorite wife. This was indeed an honor. But Maacah was an idol worshiper. It is said that she encouraged her husband to worship idols. She bore him four sons: Abijah, Attai, Ziza, and Shelomith.

Maacah met her Waterloo when her grandson King Asa turned to God and began to walk in His ways after Ahijah the prophet counseled him. King Asa did what was right in the eyes of the Lord, as did his forefather David (1 Kings 15:11). Asa banished the perverted people from the land and removed all the idols that his father had made, without exception. Because his grandmother Maacah did not adhere to this new ruling and insisted on making an obscene image of Asherah, a Phoenician goddess whose worship was lewd and associated with Baal, King Asa removed from her the honor of being Queen Mother. How humiliating and devastating it must have been for Maacah to be reprimanded by her own grandson because of her evildoing. One would think it would be the other way around.

# NOADIAH

*Nehemiah 6:14*

Noadiah was a woman who is known only by the company she kept.

"My God, think thou upon Tobiah and Sanballat according to their works, and on the prophetess Noadiah and the rest of the prophets, that would have put me in fear" (Nehemiah 6:14). This is a prayer prayed by Nehemiah. He was speaking about three troublemakers he had encountered.

Nehemiah 6:14 is the only Scripture in the Bible that mentions Noadiah's name. There is no information on her genealogy or the position she held, other than the fact that she is referred to as a prophetess. But we do know who her sidekicks were. Tobiah was an Ammonite who did not want to see the Jews return to rebuild the walls around the city of Jerusalem. Neither did Sanballat, a Horonite, the governor of the territory. Tobiah and Sanballat had worked together for months to prevent this from happening. Given the context of Nehemiah's prayer, I think it is safe to assume that Noadiah was against the work, too. She was considered a prophetess, but she was like Baalam: on the wrong side—against God's people.

It is a good thing to stand for something, but be very sure that what you are standing for is noble and worthy of a good reputation.

# VASHTI

*Esther 1 and 2*

The name Vashti means "beautiful woman." Vashti must have been one of the most beautiful women in the territory of Persia when King Ahasuerus ruled. The king thought so much of her physical beauty—for she was fair to look upon—that he wanted to show her off at a drinking festival. It was a custom in the East that women never associated with men in public. This is why, during this event, the men were in the garden court and the women were having a feast in the royal house.

After drinking wine for seven days, the king found that his heart was very merry. He commanded that Queen Vashti come into the garden court so that he may display her beauty to his intoxicated guests. The queen's sense of dignity and modesty was offended. She refused to obey her husband, the king. She was very brave. She knew that her refusal might cost her crown and, perhaps, her life. Regardless, she was determined not to expose herself to the lustful gazes of these men. Her refusal was seen as contempt for the king, wronging him in front of all his friends and dignitaries, and setting a dangerous example (i.e., encouraging all women to disobey their husbands). If the king did not reprimand her, then her behavior would be seen as a new precedent—and his power over his household and his kingdom would be weakened. As a result, Vashti was banished from her position as queen and replaced by another, Esther.

Vashti was not a bad queen. It was the providence of God that she be removed to make way for His chosen people. She bowed out gracefully, not realizing she was being used by God.

Vashti's dignity and self-respect were more valuable to her than her husband's lofty kingdom and his great wealth. Rather than submit to the lustful gaze of drunkards, she boldly gave up her position as queen of the world's leading kingdom. Rather than lower her standard of modesty, she chose dishonor and banishment.

**She might appear to some as a loser, but the true winner in the drunken court that day was the woman who refused to expose herself, even though the king had commanded her to do so.**

Vashti's action is an example for all Christian women today to follow. Do not go anywhere,look at, touch, or say, eat, drink, wear, or listen to anything, that is demeaning to your high calling in life. Be strong in the Lord and in the power of His might. Maintain a standard that will inspire others to respect you for the content of your character, and not your sexual identity..

"Better a good name than riches" (Proverbs 22:1).

# ESTHER

*Esther 1–10*

The name Hadassah, used only once in the Bible (in Esther 2:7), is translated as "Esther." Esther was the daughter of Abihail, whose nephew Mordecai was an official in the court of King Xerxes ("Ahasuerus" in Hebrew). Upon her parents' death, Esther was adopted by Mordecai, her cousin, and was raised as his own daughter.

One notable thing about the book of Esther is that, like in the Song of Solomon, God is not mentioned at all. But the providence of God is seen throughout the book as He miraculously saves His people by leading Esther to the throne.

This story takes place about fifty years after Cyrus had signed a decree permitting the Jews to return to Jerusalem. After that first deportation, only about fifty thousand returned. Many remained in Persia because they were established there. Some had houses and land, businesses, etc. The seventy-year captivity was just as the term implies: they were captives, not slaves like the Israelites of Egypt. The Jews had much more freedom in Babylon/Persia as captives than the Hebrew had had in Egypt as slaves. Many of the captives had died, and those remaining, who were under seventy years of age, (70 years were the length of their captivity) did not know what it had been like in Jerusalem, anyway. Although they had heard the story. Their captivity was the only life they knew.

In the days when King Ahasuerus was king of Persia (486–465 BC), ruling over 127 provinces from India to Ethiopia, he held a feast for all of his kingdom's officials and servants. The feast lasted 180 days. After that one, Ahasuerus held another feast—for seven days and for all the people, great and small—in Shushan Palace. On the seventh day, when he and all of his guests were thoroughly drunk with wine, he thought about Vashti, his most beautiful queen. He instructed his seven eunuchs to bring Vashti to the feast so he could show her off to his drunken guests. Vashti refused to obey his command. She would not subject herself to low, indignant stares and exposure. She possessed too much purity of character and self-respect to be a participant in such a degrading thing. . So she refused and thereby disobeyed her husband's command, knowing full well what the consequences of her actions would be. The king was greatly offended and much grieved. So, with the counsel of his staff, he banished Vashti from the kingdom and divorced her.

The queen now had to be replaced. Ahasuerus began a search throughout his entire kingdom for beautiful, young virgins. Mordecai encouraged his beautiful niece, Esther to enter the contest. And she did. She was instructed not to reveal her nationality. When the contest was concluded, Esther was chosen as queen. King Ahasuerus considered her the most beautiful contender of the competition. He was very pleased with her. Esther submitted to a full year of preparation to become the first lady of the land. Her attendants left nothing undone so as to enhance her beauty and charm. She became Ahasuerus's pride and joy. With him she was blessed and highly favored.

Scripture does not tell us just how much time passed before a controversy arose. Esther's uncle Mordecai was one of the king's gatekeepers. One day, he overheard disgruntled servants discussing a plot to kill the king. He sent a message to Esther, and Esther revealed it to the king. The plot was crushed and the would-be assassins were hanged.

About the same time, coincidentally, Haman was promoted to the highest position in the kingdom next to the king. Haman became chief minister. All of the king's servants who were within the kingdom's gate bowed and paid homage to Haman when he passed, but Mordecai refrained from doing so. Mordecai considered such a thing to be a form of worship. He knew that the law of God clearly instructed people to have no other gods before Jehovah/ Yahweh and admonished them not to bow down before or serve anyone else.

Mordecai's refusal to bow down angered Haman and aroused his hatred for not only Mordecai, but also all Jews. Haman set out to destroy all of the Jews. But he did this in an underhanded way. He wrote a draft of a law and convinced the king to sign it. Evidently, the king didn't even read it because he greatly trusted Haman. The law stated that on a certain date, the citizens of the country could kill all the Jews they wished and confiscate their belongings, making them their own.

Mordecai heard about this and sent a message to Queen Esther, asking her to appeal to the king on her people's behalf. After all, if they perished, she would eventually be discovered and perish also. He closed with the question, "Who knows that thou has come to the kingdom for such a time as this?"

Esther was greatly distressed. She sent a message back to Mordecai with a request that all Jews fast for her for three days. Then she would go to the king. If she perished, then she perished. The Scripture does not mention that she prayed, but since prayer and fasting usually go together, It is assumed that Esther and her people prayed as well as fasted.

The Jews complied with Esther's request. After three days, Esther, by faith, went to see the king uninvited, which was against the royal rules. The king extended his scepter in acceptance of her, so Esther was safe. The king asked her, "What is your wish up to half of my kingdom?" He was in a really good mood. This is evidence of what prayer and fasting can do. Esther invited the king and his right-hand man, Haman, to a banquet. Both men accepted.

At the banquet, Esther did not reveal her real concern. Instead, she set a date for another banquet. Both men agreed to attend. Haman now thought he was earning points with the new queen. On his way home, he encountered Mordecai and his blood began to boil, as it were. Once home, he vented himself to his wife and friends. They suggested that he build a seventy-five-foot gallows and have Mordecai hung. Haman accepted their erroneous counsel and proceeded to follow through.

At the next banquet, Esther dropped a bombshell. She pleaded with the king to annul the law that had been established to destroy her and all her people (the Jews). The king's reply was, "Who is he, and where is he, who would dare presume in his heart to do such a thing?" And Esther said, "The adversary and enemy is this wicked Haman!" Haman had put into law a decree that would destroy all the Jews in the kingdom, of whom she was one. The king, furious, stood to his feet and sentenced Haman to be hung on the same seventy-five-foot gallows he had constructed for Mordecai. Then Mordecai was promoted to Haman's position.

"For Mordecai was great in the king's palace and his fame spread throughout all the provinces; for this man Mordecai waxed greater and greater" (Esther 9:4). Mordecai the Jew was second to King Ahasuerus and was great among the Jews. He was well received by the multitude of his brethren. He sought the good of his people and spoke peace to all his countrymen (Esther 10:3).

Esther pleaded with her husband the king to annul the decree of Haman which would annihilate the Jews. The king informed her that any law that is signed with the king's name and sealed with the king's ring cannot be reversed. But the king authorized Mordecai to put into effect another law that would counteract

Haman's law. The king granted the Jews which were in every city to gather themselves together, and to stand for their lives, to destroy, to slay and to cause to perish all the power of the people and province that would assault them, both little ones and women and to take the spoil of them for a prey. And the slaughter was great. The Jews slew thousands

This occasion is celebrated today in the Jewish religion. It is called Purim, from the root word *pur*, which means "to cast lots." (Haman had cast lots to determine the date of the proposed holocaust.) The Jews celebrate Purim every year on the fourteenth of March as a memorial of Haman's failed plot to destroy the Jews and of Queen Esther's miraculous success in saving her people.

"When the wicked are multiplied, transgression increases, but the righteous will see their fall" (Proverbs 29:16).

# ZERESH

*Esther 5:10, 14; 6:13; 7:9, 10; 9:10, 14*

Zeresh was the wife of Haman the Agagite, who was the head advisor to King Xerxes ("Ahasuerus" in Hebrew). Haman had problems with Mordecai, who was a Jewish gatekeeper in a Persian kingdom. Haman simply thought that Mordecai didn't give him the respect he deserved. Mordecai did not stand and bow to Haman when he passed, like the other gatekeepers did. After Haman talked to his wife, Zeresh, and to his friends, they advised him to build a gallows fifty feet high and have Mordecai hanged on it. But through a twist of fate, the tables were turned. Haman was hung on the gallows he had built for Mordecai. Soon after that, Haman's ten sons were killed also.

Try to imagine, if you will, how awfully grieved Zeresh must have been about losing her husband and her sons. And just to think that she had a part in this evil decision that prompted their tragic deaths. If she had been a peacemaker like Abagail, then perhaps she could have saved her husband's life as well as the lives of her ten sons, who were executed later in connection with the same incident. Zeresh had to live with that sorrow and guilt for the remainder of her life.

"Be not overcome with evil, but overcome evil with good" (Romans 12:21).

"Whoso diggeth a pit for someone else shall fall there, and he that rolleth a stone, it will return upon him" (Proverbs 26:27).

# JOB'S DAUGHTERS JEMIMA; KEZIA, AND KERENHAPPUCH

*Job 42:12-15*

After Job had gone through his great ordeal, he emerged victoriously. God restored what Job had lost, doubling the material possessions he previously owned. God also gave Job another set of children, seven boys and three girls. These girls were the fairest in all the land. Their names were Jemima, Kezia, and Kerenhappuch. Nothing is said about Job's wife or the names of his seven sons. I wonder why.

The emphasis in the Scripture is on the three girls who were the fairest in all the land. Many of the later Bible translators automatically interpret the word *fair* to mean "physically beautiful." This puts a limitation on the word. Given the context in which it is stated, its meaning has to be something more profound than that. First Samuel 16:7 states, "Man looketh on the outward appearance, but God looketh on the heart."

The word *fair* has other meanings, including "just," "equitable," "of flawless quality," "clean," "pure," "free from selfishness," "marked by impartiality," "honest," "righteous," and "open to legitimate pursuit." We would do well to consider both interpretations; external and internal beauty. Did Job's three daughters possess outward beauty? Yes. Did they possess internal beauty? Most assuredly.

The names Job gave his daughters evidently had meanings. The only meanings I found for the three daughters' names come from Matthew Henry's commentary. They are as follows:

- Jemima – "Day." It was now daytime for Job. He had been living in perpetual night with the darkness of adversity, temporal and spiritual, but now he enjoyed prosperity, spiritual light, and joy.

- Kezia, or Cassia – "An herb of sweet smell." Unlike living with the stench of his breath and body, which had been very offensive, Job was now free of odor.

- Kerenhappuch – "Horn of paint" or "horn turned." Opposite to his horn's being defiled in the dust and his face's being fouled with weeping, Job had experienced a sudden turn in his condition.

Job's troubles began with Satan's malice, which God restrained; his restoration began with God's mercy, which Satan could not restrain. Job's fortune changed when he prayed for his friends, not when he was disputing with them (Job 42:10). The lesson here is that God does not hold you accountable for how people treat you, but He does hold you accountable for how you treat others.

I submit that the names and characters of these three fair daughters are a memorial to their father's great trial and subsequent victory.

# GOMER

*Hosea 3:1-5*

Gomer's father's name was Diblaim. Gomer was a prostitute. God commanded Hosea to marry her, and he did. She became notorious for her infidelity. Though married, she carried on numerous illicit love affairs.

Gomer's name means "completion"; that is, the filling up of the cup of idolatry. Her name was symbolic of the adultery and idolatry of the kingdom she represented. Hers was a life of whoredom. She was of the northern kingdom and her story is a living human allegory - a symbol of her people, the Israelites.

Gomer gave birth to three children. God gave her the names for each of her children. These names were indicative of his relationship with the people of that kingdom. Gomer's three children were as follows:

1. A son, Jezreel, meaning "God soweth"

2. A daughter, Lo-Ruhamah, meaning "No more mercy"

3. A son, Lo-am-mi, meaning, "You are not My people, and I will not be your God"

Hosea represents God the Father, and Gomer represents the church. Her life of adultery and infidelity is a vivid and dramatic example of our modern-day life of spiritual adultery and unfaithfulness. That Hosea redeemed Gomer from the auction block mirrors how Christ redeems us from Satan's execution and restores us to a right relationship with God.

Dr. G. Campbell Morgan wrote,

> Out of his own heart agony Hosea learned the nature of the sin of his people. They were playing the harlot, spending God's gifts in lewd traffic with other lovers. Out of that agony he has learned how God suffers over the sin of His people because of His undying love. Out of God's love Hosea's new care for Gomer was born, and in the method God ordained for him with her, he discovered God's method with Israel. Out of all this process of pain, there came full confidence in the ultimate victory of love. Thus equipped, he delivers his messages and all through them will sound those deep notes of Sin, Love and Hope.[1]

Only God could turn such a negative experience into a positive lesson. The story of Hosea and Gomer is a true metaphor of God's love for His wayward people-meaning you and I.

---

[1]        G. Campbell Morgan, *The Minor Prophets* (New York: Fleming H. Revell Co., 1909).

# New Testament Woman

The Bible consists of sixty-six books. The last twenty-seven were written after Christ came to earth and are referred to as the New Testament. There are many women mentioned in this testament. Also, the transition from the Jewish to the Christian religion and all the conflicts that it presented are introduced in the New Testament. The stories indicate that women had more of an integral part to play in the functioning of the church. Jesus as well as His disciples were assisted by and supported by many women who were part of the church. In and age when women were regarded as second- class citizens in society and in religious tradition, Jesus esteems women and allows them to play a vital role in His life, death, burial and resurrection. We also hear the apostle Paul commending these women on many occasions. It was a *new era* for women; a new day had dawned bringing with it new privileges and opportunities.

# ELISABETH

*Luke 1:5-80*

In the days of King Herod of Judea, there was a priest named Zacharias whose wife's name was Elisabeth. The couple were righteous before God, walking blamelessly and following all of the Lord's commandments and ordinances. But they had no child, because Elizabeth was barren. They were both well advanced in years. One day, while Zacharias was serving as priest before God, an angel appeared to him. When Zacharias saw the angel, he was troubled and fear fell upon him. But the angel said to him, "Do not be afraid, for your prayer is heard; and your wife Elizabeth will bear you a son, and you shall call his name John. And he shall be great in the sight of the Lord ... and shall be filled with the Holy Spirit even from his mother's womb" (Luke 1:13).

Zacharias, being old and human, did what many of us would do: he asked the Lord for proof. God gave him a sign: Zacharias would be mute/dumb until the child was born. And it happened just the way the angel promised. As the angel stated to Abraham when discussing the birth of Isaac, "Is anything too hard for God?"

In the sixth month of Elisabeth's pregnancy, the angel Gabriel appeared to Elisabeth's cousin, Mary, in Nazareth and announced to her that she would be a mother. Mary, overwhelmed with joy, hurried to Elisabeth's home in Judah. Kitty Culwell wrote, "These two highly favored women, an old woman and her young cousin, had a common experience and bond that knew no age. Every step of the journey must have been in joyous anticipation of the confidences they would share with each other."[1]

When Elisabeth heard the voice of her cousin, the baby leaped in her womb and Elisabeth was filled with the Holy Spirit.

About three months after Mary returned home, Elisabeth gave birth. Her friends and relatives probably thought that she would name the child Zacharias, after his aged father. But Elisabeth said that his name would be John. Since Zacharias's voice had not yet returned, perhaps he took a pen and confirmed the name by writing. Immediately thereafter, his speech returned. With a healthy baby, John, in her arms, and with her husband, Zacharias, who was now able to verbally communicate again, by her side, Elisabeth must have felt very happy and fulfilled!

What outstanding recognition it was for Elisabeth, the mother of John the Baptist, when Jesus, near the end of John's life, perhaps after John's mother was deceased, said, "Verily I say unto you, among them that are born of women, there hath not risen a greater than John the Baptist" (Matthew 11:11). Elisabeth had done her job well.

---

[1]     Kitty Jones Culwell, *Sarah's Daughters* (Murfreesboro: DeHoff Publications, 1980).

# MARY, MOTHER OF JESUS

*Matthew 1–2; 12:46*
*Luke 1:2*
*John 2:1–11; 19:25*
*Acts 1:14*

Mary was a virgin Jewess who lived in Nazareth in the province of Galilee. She was betrothed (engaged) to Joseph, a Jewish man of the house of David. Actually, both Joseph and Mary descended from David. Prior to David, they shared the same genealogy. Mary's branch of David's family tree can be traced through David's son Nathan, while Joseph's branch is of the royal line, through Solomon. One of the main purposes of Mary and Joseph's betrothal/engagement was to test the fidelity of both partners.

During the period of Mary's betrothal to Joseph, which by custom was to precede the wedding by a year, the angel Gabriel appeared to her and said, "Rejoice, highly favored one, the Lord is with you; blessed are you among women!" This startled Mary. Then the angel said, "Be not afraid, Mary, for you have found favor with God. And behold you will conceive in your womb and bring forth a Son, and shall call His name Jesus."

"How can this be, since I do not know a man?" Mary asked. The angel explained to her that the Holy Spirit would come upon her; the power of the Most High would overshadow her; and the Holy One born of her would be called the Son of God. He proceeded to tell her that her barren cousin Elisabeth had conceived in her old age and would also bear a son. Elisabeth was now in her sixth month of pregnancy. With God, nothing is impossible. Mary said, "Let it be to me according to your word." Her reply indicates her humility and her submissiveness to godly leading. The angel departed after Mary spoke those words.

Mary arose immediately and made haste to visit her cousin in the city of Judea. And what a joyous visit it was. When Elisabeth heard the voice of Mary, the baby leaped within her womb. Then Elisabeth said, "Blessed are you among women, and blessed is the fruit of your womb."

Mary was so overjoyed that she began praising God in song, her words profound and beautiful. Her song has been set to music and is known to us today as the " **Magnificat",** which follows:

> My soul magnifies the Lord,
>
> And my spirit has rejoiced in God my Savior.
>
> For He has regarded the lowly state of His maidservant;
>
> For behold, henceforth all generations will call me blessed.
>
> For He who is mighty has done great things for me, And holy is His name.
>
> And His mercy is on those who fear Him From generation to generation.
>
> He has shown strength with His arm;

He has scattered the proud in the imagination
of their hearts.

He has put down the mighty from their
thrones, And exalted the lowly.

He has filled the hungry with good things,

And the rich He has sent away empty. He has
helped His servant Israel,

In remembrance of His mercy, As He spoke to
our fathers,

To Abraham and to his seed forever.

—Luke 1:46–55

The song is about God's goodness, His glory, His strength, and
His faithfulness throughout the ages.

Many godly women, all the way back to Eve—who had received
the promise of a Savior in the garden of Eden—had the hope of
being chosen as the one through whom the Savior would come.
But this grand privilege came to Mary—and at a high cost. She
was stigmatized as an unwed mother. Although she had remained
a virgin, and maintained her fidelity to Joseph, her friends and
neighbors were inclined to think otherwise.

Just think how awfully disappointed Joseph must have been
when he discovered that his wife-to-be was pregnant. Being the
godly man that he was—the one whom God had chosen to be
Jesus's earthly father—he thought to put Mary away quietly to
save her the embarrassment. After all, he did care about her. But
no! said the angel in a dream. "Joseph, son of David, do not be
afraid to take to you Mary your wife, for that which is conceived
in her is of the Holy Spirit. And she will bring forth a Son, and

you shall call His name Jesus, for He will save His people **from** their sins."

But when the fullness of time had come, God sent forth His Son, born of a woman, born under the law, to redeem those who were under the law, that we might be adopted as His sons and daughters (Galatians 4:4–5).

Jesus was nourished, fed, clothed, and taught by Mary and Joseph in their humble home. Luke 2:52 says, "And Jesus increased in <u>wisdom</u> (mentally)and <u>stature (physically)</u> and in <u>favor with God (spiritually)</u> and <u>man (socially)</u>." These are the four (4) dimensions in the composition of man.

After Jesus's babyhood, we see Mary interacting with Him on only four occasions:

1. At the Passover when He was twelve years old (Luke 2)

2. At a wedding feast (John 2)

3. While He was teaching His disciples (Mark 3)

4. At His crucifixion (John 19:25–27)

As a Man, Jesus was Mary's son, but as God, He was her Lord. One of His last earthly acts before yielding up His life was to ensure that His mother would be cared for. In His final hours, already in the throes of death, He saw Mary with teary eyes standing near to John, His beloved disciple. Jesus said, "Woman, behold your son, and son behold your mother." That same day, John took Mary to his own home.

This final act bespeaks of Mary's relationship with her son. She was His earthly mother, but He was her eternal God. She understood and accepted that relationship. She bowed to His authority in heavenly matters, just as, in His childhood, He had been subject to her parental authority in earthly matters. As a mother, she had once provided all His earthly needs, but in the ultimate and spiritual sense, He was now her Savior and provided her salvation.

There is no record in sacred scripture of Mary claiming or professing to be anything more than a meek and lowly handmaiden of the Lord. She is presented in Scripture as the humble instrument whom God used to be the mother of His Son. She was extraordinary because God used her in an extraordinary way.

God has a purpose and a plan for each of us. We need only to submit to Him as ordinary people and He will transform us into extraordinary people.

# ANNA

*Luke 2:36–38*

Anna is the same name as Hanna in the Old Testament. The name means "favor" or "grace." Anna was the daughter of Phanuel, the same as Penuel in the Old Testament, which name means "face or appearance of God." Anna's father was of the tribe of Asher. Interestingly, she is the only person of note mentioned in the New Testament from the tribe of Asher; the name Asher means "blessedness."

Anna served in the temple day and night, maybe something like a nun. We do not know exactly. But it appears that she was there most of the time. Her life was absorbed in the service of God; she had no other interests to distract her attention. She was a widow, eighty-four years old.

Anna was also a prophetess, one who received and delivered messages from God to the people. At the time of Mary's and Joseph's visit to the temple for baby Jesus's blessing, Simeon was the priest. When Simeon blessed the Baby Jesus, he recognized Him as the Christ Child and prophesized that He was. Anna heard him and rejoiced, for at last the Messiah had come. As she gazed upon the face of the babe of Bethlehem, she knew that the past predictions of His coming were fulfilled and her wait was over. Along with Simeon, she believed that this babe was indeed the promised Redeemer, or Messiah.

Anna gave thanks (and praise) to the Lord and continued to speaks of him to those who looked for redemption in Jerusalem. Previously, Anna had spoken of the prophecies that pointed forward to the coming of the Messiah; now, she could speak from personal experience about the fact that the Messiah had come, as she had seen Him with her own eyes.

Is it your personal experience that the Messiah has come into your life?

# SALOME

*Matthew 20:20–23; 27:55, 56*
*Mark 15:40–41; 16:1–8*

Salome was the wife of Zebedee, a fisherman, and the mother of James and John, two of Jesus's most notable disciples. One tradition has it that she was Mary's sister, Jesus's aunt. Salome and Zebedee lived in Capernaum, the town where Jesus dwelled during most of His ministry. Capernaum was located at the northern end of the Sea of Galilee.

Salome was one of the dedicated women who followed Jesus and ministered to His needs. She might have been one of His earliest converts. When her sons were called from their fishing boat to follow Jesus (they had a lucrative business), there is no record of any objections from either Zebedee or Salome.

Salome was with Jesus at the cross. She was with Him at the tomb, too, and probably at the ascension.

There is only one selfish thing mentioned about Salome's character in Scriptures. One day, she came to Jesus with a special request. He asked her, "What do you wish?" She said to Him, "Grant that my two sons may sit one on Your right and the other on the left when you enter your kingdom." Her lack of understanding, along with the lack of understanding of all the disciples, was very disappointing to Jesus. Jesus said to her, "You do not know what you ask. Are they able to drink of the cup that I shall drink of, and be baptized with the baptism that I am baptized with?"

It seems as though none of Jesus's followers understood His mission or His kingdom until after they experienced Pentecost. Even after He told them that His kingdom was not of this world, they continued to look for an earthly king to sit on David's earthly throne and be a physical deliverer. They had always dealt in earthly things. Their spiritual understanding had not yet been activated. At that point in time, they were walking by sight and not by faith.

In the end, Salome's two sons did drink of the cup of persecution and were baptized with suffering. Herod reached forth with a sword and pierced through James' body. James was the first disciple to be martyred for the Christian faith. Although John was the last to die, he was exiled to the Isle of Patmos, where God came to him in vision and gave to the church, through John, the wonderful book of Revelation.

What a wonderful contribution that this mother, Salome, made to Christianity: her two sons.

# MARTHA AND MARY (MAGDALENE)

*Luke 10:38–42*
*John 11:1–46*

Martha and Mary were sisters. They had a brother named Lazarus. Their home was in Bethany, a little town about three miles outside of Jerusalem by way of Jericho Road. They were very close friends of Jesus. We have no record of how this friendship originated. Jesus spent many hours visiting with them and relaxing in their home. They always made Him feel welcome.

We have no biblical information on the background of Mary, Martha, and Lazarus, only several unverified traditions.

> One tradition has it that the family was from Magdala, a small fishing village on the coast of the sea of Galilee, then relocated to Bethany after the death of their father. Who was supposedly of royal descent of the House of David. He possessed riches and land, which were equally divided between them. Martha managed her possessions with discretion and was an example of virtue and propriety. On the contrary, Mary, perhaps a little too much addicted to worldly attractions, abandoned herself to luxurious pleasures and became at length notorious for her extravagant lifestyle that she became known

148

throughout the country as Mary of Magdala, the sinner; alias—prostitute.

We first catch a glimpse of the group in Martha's home when Jesus and His disciples were visiting there for dinner. Martha was being a gracious hostess, preparing the food, and Mary was sitting at the feet of Jesus, undistracted, absorbing every word that proceeded from His lips. But Martha, distracted with serving, said to Jesus, "Lord, do You not care that my sister has left me to serve alone? Therefore tell her to help me." Jesus's answer was a loving rebuke: "Martha, Martha, you are worried and troubled about many things. But one things is needed, and Mary has chosen that good part, which will not be taken away from her." Mary was filling her mind with the precious words of Jesus, which were more precious to her than earth's most valuable jewels. The "one thing" that Martha needed was a calm, devotional spirit, a deeper concern for spiritual knowledge concerning salvation, the graces necessary for spiritual advancement, less anxiety for the things that pass away, and more concern for things that are eternal. Jesus taught His disciples then and now to take advantage of every opportunity to gain the knowledge that would make them wise about salvation.

Martha and Mary are mentioned together only three times in Scripture. Martha is not mentioned again. As Mary Magdalene, Mary is mentioned fourteen times. Eight times, she is mentioned with other women, but her name always leads the list, which indicates that she was the leader of the group. Five times, she is mentioned alone in association with the death and resurrection of Jesus. In one case, her name is mentioned second to the mother of our Lord. She was one of Jesus's most devoted disciples.

On another occasion, Martha's and Mary's brother, Lazarus, became gravely ill. They had, no doubt, seen Jesus heal the sick many times, so they sent Him a message: "Lord, he whom you love is ill." They were sure He would come, but He did not arrive.

So they sent another message. But He still didn't come. Lazarus's death came instead. After their brother died, Jesus came. He knew that the house would be full of mourners, natural and paid, so He stopped a little ways back, remained out of sight, and sent for Martha, who ran to meet Him. Upon seeing Him, she spoke a rebuke to Him: "Lord, if you had been here, my brother would not have died, but even now I know that whatever you ask from God, God will give you." These words bespeak a mixture of grief and faith. Jesus said to Martha, "I am the resurrection and the life; he who believes in Me, though he dies, yet shall he live; and whosoever lives and believes in me shall never die. Do you believe this?" Martha's answer was truly a confession of her faith: "Yea, Lord, I believe that thou are the Christ, the Son of God, which should come into the world."

Martha ran back to the house and announced to Mary that their friend Jesus had come and was asking for her. Mary made haste to meet Him. She fell down at His feet, repeating the very same words that Martha had said: "Lord, if you had been here, my brother would not have died."

Observing the sadness and grief surrounding Lazarus's death, "Jesus wept" (John 11:35), which is the shortest verse in the Bible. Jesus loved Lazarus. But His grief was caused not so much by the death of Lazarus as by the unbelief and hardness of the heart of some of the people who were in the crowd of mourners.

Jesus instructed some among the mourners to remove the stone. Martha was hesitant to permit this. She said, "He has been dead for four days; he stinks now." Martha was very conscious of doing things the proper way; she had finesse.

After the stone was removed, Jesus said in a loud voice, "Lazarus, come forth." The people heard the rumbling in the tomb and then saw Lazarus come forth in his grave clothes. Jesus said, "Loose him and let him go."

The third and last time we see Martha and Mary together is at their uncle Simon's house. There seems to have been a joint celebration; Jesus had healed Simon of leprosy and had raised Lazarus from the dead. Again, Martha was doing the thing she liked best: serving food. And Mary was doing what she liked best: sitting at the feet of Jesus. But this time, Mary was not sitting quietly. She washed Jesus's feet with her tears and then dried them with her hair. Perhaps no one really noticed until they smelled the sophisticated aroma of the expensive spikenard perfume filling the room. Scriptures tell us that the price of the spikenard was three hundred pence. The wage at that time was about one pence per day, so the spikenard represented about a year's labor. But to Mary, nothing was too good for her Lord.

Some criticized Mary for anointing Jesus with the expensive ointment, but Jesus praised her for her gift. "Let her alone; against the day of my burial she has done this" (Matthew 26:13). Simon, Jesus's host, had been influenced by the criticism, which was led by Judas, Simon's son, (John 6:71). In his heart, Simon questioned, *If this man is a prophet, would not He know that this woman who touches Him is a sinner?* By curing Simon of leprosy, Christ had saved him from a living death. But now Simon questioned whether the Savior was really no more than a prophet. Jesus, reading the nonverbal thoughts of Simon's heart, answered him verbally. He said, "Simon, I have somewhat to say unto thee. There was a certain creditor which had two debtors: the one owed five hundred pence, and the other fifty. And when they had nothing to pay, he frankly forgave them both. Tell Me therefore, which of them will love the most."

Simon answered, "I suppose that he, to whom he forgave most." And Jesus said to Simon, "Thou has rightly judged." Now Simon saw Jesus as who He really was. While Simon thought that he was reading his guest, his guest had been reading him.

Mary had been looked upon as a great sinner, but Christ knew the circumstances that had caused her to sin. Seven times, He had lifted her from despair and ruin (Luke 8:2). On one occasion, He healed her along with two other women, Joanna, wife of Chuza, Herod's steward, and Susanna, who also became one of Christ's followers (Luke 8:3). Ellen White wrote in Desire of Ages.

> The one who had fallen, and whose mind had been a habitation of demons, was brought very near to the Savior in fellowship and ministry. It was Mary who sat at His feet and learned of Him. It was Mary who poured upon His head the precious anointing oil and bathed His feet with her tears. Mary stood beside the cross and followed Him to the sepulcher. Mary was first at the tomb after His resurrection. It was Mary who first proclaimed a risen Savior.

John MacArthur wrote in Extraordinary Women.

> Martha was a noble and godly woman with a servant's heart and a rare capacity for work. Mary was nobler still, with an unusual predisposition for worship and wisdom. Both were remarkable in their own ways. If we weigh their gifts and their instincts together, they give us a wonderful example to follow. May we diligently cultivate the best qualities of both of these extraordinary women.

# MARY AND MARY

*Matthew 27:55–61*
*Mark 15:40, 47; 16:1*
*Luke 23:49–56; 24:10*

## Mary, Mother of James and Joses

We know very little about this Mary. Some say that she was the wife of Cleopas or Alphaeus. But one thing we are pretty sure about: she was the mother of two sons, James and Joses. One of her sons was chosen by Jesus to join His disciples. We know him as " James the Less", to distinguish him from James the Just, the brother of John.

Mary was among the women who followed Jesus to the cross and witnessed His death. She was with the other women who carried spices to the tomb to anoint His body, only to discover that He wasn't there but had risen, just as He had said He would. It is believed that in addition to giving her son, Mary gave of her time and means to minister to Jesus and His disciples as a token of her love.

## Mary, Mother of John Mark

*Acts 12:1–19*

Mary, the mother of John Mark who wrote the book of Mark, is spoken of but once in the Bible. But this brief description of her is suggestive of her life and labors. We see Peter at her house when he is released from prison after intercessory prayer was made on his behalf.

Mary's son John Mark was first introduced to gospel work by his cousin Barnabas when he was on a mission trip with Paul. He was not impressed at first and returned home to his mother. Neither was Paul impressed with him. This caused a split in the relationship of Barnabus and Paul. John Mark worked with Barnabus on his next mission trip. Paul chose Timothy on his next mission trip . Still, John Mark didn't give up. He proved to be a very fine minister. In many of Paul's letters, we hear him speaking of John Mark as his son. During Paul's final incarceration, he specifically requested that John Mark come to minister to him.

Later on, John Mark worked with Peter as an assistant evangelist. It is said by some scholars and agreed by others that Peter dictated the information to John Mark, who then wrote it down and presented it as the book we know today as the Gospel of Mark.

One never knows what a person may become with a little love and patience, especially when he or she has a godly mother.

# LYDIA

*Acts 15:36–18:22*

Lydia's story is quite an intriguing one. She is best remembered as the seller of purple who was the original European convert to the gospel. Lydia was born in the city of Thyatira, in the province of Lydia, which was home to one of the seven churches described in Revelation, Chapters 2 and 3. Thyatira was located in the very region of Asia Minor where, Luke tells us, Paul, Silas, and Timothy were forbidden by the Holy Spirit to preach the Word (Acts 16:5–7).

The providential hand of God was guiding this group, although they did not realize it at that time. Every door of ministry in Asia had been closed to them for evangelism. That's when Paul received the dream in which a man stood and pleaded, saying "Come over to Macedonia and help us." God was making it perfectly clear to them that there was just one way ahead, Macedonia. They made haste to follow His leading.

Philippi was a prosperous cosmopolitan city with lots of businesses and merchants from all over the world. It was the perfect location for introducing the gospel to Europe.

Paul's usual procedure was to take the gospel to the synagogue first. If he went to the Gentiles first, then the Jews would not listen to what he had to say. But there were no synagogues in

Philippi. There were only a few Jews in Philippi, not enough to support a synagogue.

According to Jewish tradition, Jewish women in communities without synagogues could pray together in groups if they liked, but men had to form a quorum of ten before they could partake in any kind of formal, public worship, including prayer, the reading of the Torah, and the giving of public blessings. So Paul, hearing of this, sought to learn the location of the place where the women usually gathered and then invited himself there. The women welcomed him. Evidently, this was the only public gathering of Philippian Jews who met on the Sabbath day. As Paul preached, the one woman who responded most eagerly was not Jewish, but a Gentile convert to Judaism. Acts 16:14 says, "Now a certain woman named Lydia heard us. She was a seller of purple from the city of Thyatira, who worshiped God. The Lord opened her heart to heed the things spoken by Paul." "Lydia heard us" means that she listened intently, not with her ears only but also with her heart. As a result, she accepted the gospel of Jesus Christ.

Lydia was a businesswoman who sold purple dye and fancy purple cloth that was made by a famous guild in her hometown of Thyatira. Her cloth was worn and used by the well-to-do. She had her own home and a family with servants. She not only became a believer in Christ herself, but she also influenced her household to come to Christ.

Lydia was hospitable. She invited the missionary party to live in her house during their stay in Philippi. Lydia was a businesswoman, her house was big enough to accommodate the missionary team to stay overnight, that she had servants. All this seemed to indicate that she was a woman of economic means.

Lydia's story is an example of remarkable faith. Because she opened her heart and her home, the gospel gained a solid foothold in

Philippi. It was from this small beginning, from the house of Lydia, that the gospel of Jesus Christ spread all over Europe.

I think it is safe to say that Lydia was not slothful in business. Instead, she was fervent in spirit in her service to the Lord. She was a woman who gave her heart, her home, and her means to the uplifting of the gospel of Jesus Christ.

# SAPPHIRA

*Acts 5:1–11*

In the early days of the Christian church, soon after Pentecost, the spirit of liberality was very strong. The unspoken rule of selling some of one's possessions and donating the funds to the church to help further the cause was expressed by some. Thinking it a good idea, others soon joined in. A certain couple named Ananias and Sapphira vowed to donate to the church, too. Remember, this was not a requirement, but a strictly voluntary act. This couple sold their property, agreeing between themselves to take only half the funds to the church. When Ananias brought his money to the feet of Peter, the apostle Peter, being filled with the Holy Ghost, asked him why he would lie to God. Then Ananias fell dead and was taken out and buried.

Three hours later, Ananias's wife, Sapphira, came in. Peter inquired of her if she and her husband had received a certain amount for the land—the amount Ananias had reported. Sapphira verified the figure. Peter said, "How is it that you have agreed together to test the Spirit of the Lord? Look, the feet of those who have buried your husband are at the door, and they will carry you out." Sapphira immediately fell down at Peter's feet and breathed her last breath.

As stated by Ellen white in, Acts of the Apostles, pp. 72-74. "But God hates hypocrisy and falsehood. Ananias and Sapphira practice fraud in their dealing with God; they lied to the Holy Spirit, and their sin was visited with swift and terrible judgment... Infinite Wisdom say that this signal manifestation of the wrath of God was necessary to guard the young church from becoming demoralized. Their numbers were rapidly increasing. The church would have been endangered if, in the rapid increase of converts, men and women had been added who, while professing to serve God, were worshiping mammon. This judgment testified that men cannot deceive God, that He detects the hidden sin of the heart and that He will not be mocked.......From the stern punishment meted out to those perjurers, God would have us learn also how deep is His hatred and contempt for all hypocrisy and deception."

Sapphira was as guilty as her husband. She was aware of all of the transactions they had made. The evil was committed with her knowledge and support. Some believe that It might have even been her suggestion to deceive the Church leaders..

Some commentators suggest, and I am inclined to agree, that just as Satan sought to ruin God's original creation by eliciting the disobedience of earth's first pair, Adam and Eve, he became active again, this time through a different couple, Ananias and Sapphira, to destroy God's new creation, His blood-bought church. Sapphira and her husband had cast the first trace of a shadow upon the young church when they agreed to tempt the Lord. The satanically motivated deception of these two who agreed together to lie to God was the first recorded act of deception within the newly formed Christian church. Hence, Ananais's and Sapphira's severe punishments were justified.

The love of money is the root of all kinds of evil. Sapphira, like many Christian women of today, yesterday, and the future, was not, is not and will not be able to stand a stern test involving honesty in money.

Knowing that God's all-seeing eyes see all things, may we live and walk in the light, having lives that are clear and transparent.

"It is better not to vow than to vow and not pay" (Ecclesiastes 5:5).

# Dorcas

*Acts 9:36–42*

Just seven little verses in the book of Acts
Tell a wonderful story with many facts.
In the town of Joppa, near the Mediterranean Sea,
Lived a Christian woman who was as busy as a bee.
She was full of good works and charitable deeds.
She was not selfish and had no greed.
She loved the Lord and His people, too.
Fulfilling their needs gave her much to do.
She made clothes without pay
And gave some people food every day.
She did more than her part.
She was a philanthropist at heart.
Unfortunately, one day she died,
And all the city came out and cried.
To them, her death was an awful blow,
So they sent for Peter in the town next door.
Peter came without delay.
When he arrived, he began to pray.

He saw widows standing and weeping.

He knew that Dorcas was in God's keeping.

He cleared the people from the room,

Then called Dorcas (also known as Tabitha) from death's tomb.

He said, "Tabitha, arise."

On hearing His words, she opened her eyes.

She thanked the Lord—and Peter, too—

For this miracle that only God could do.

Because of what was that day achieved,

Many in that town believed

In God the Father and God the Son,

And looked forward to Christ's return.

Will you be among that great number

Who, when He comes, may be in slumber

But, upon hearing the archangel, will awaken

To be with those who will be taken

To live forever with Him above

And be partakers of His love?

The Dorcas Society is known worldwide.

Its purpose is to keep Dorcas's spirit of charity alive.

BY: VERNEVA GOSS WHITE

# RHODA

*Acts 12:1–19*

Rhoda was the maidservant of Mary, who was the mother of John Mark. They lived in Jerusalem. Mary was a generous and hospitable woman who, on many occasions, had opened her home to the saints as a place of worship and for holding special meetings.

Herod the king had killed James, the brother of John, with a sword (James was the first disciple to give his life as a martyr for the Christian faith). Herod had then arrested Peter and planned to kill him also, after Easter. So he put him in prison, with six guards to watch him. Peter's hands were bound to two guards, and his feet were in chains. An all-night prayer visual was held at the house of Mary. Many saints were there, all interceding for Peter. Their prayers were miraculously answered. Peter came forth from prison, led by an angel. Peter's first stop was Mary's house.

It was after midnight when Peter arrived and knocked on the door. Rhoda ran to the door and asked who was knocking. When she heard Peter's voice, she was so elated that she forgot to open the door. Instead, she ran to the prayer room and announced to the prayer group that Peter was at the door. No one believed her. Rhoda insisted over and over that what she said was true, but to no avail. The group accused her of being mad. But she still insisted. They said, "Maybe it is his angel."

Peter was still knocking. The group reconsidered what Rhoda had said because an angel could have come in without the door's being opened. Finally, they opened the door. There stood Peter. They were astonished and overwhelmed. They invited him in, after which time he related his miraculous story.

Having Peter at the door and realizing that the group's prayer had been answered, Rhoda experienced a joy that overpowered her normal reaction of opening the door. She forgot herself and her duty. But she would not permit the others to browbeat her into silence.

O how we need Rhodas today, people who will stand up and tell the truth—even if they have to stand alone—never fearing the consequences.

# PRISCILLA

*Acts 18:1–8*
*1 Corinthians 16; 19*
*Ephesians 5:22*

Priscilla was a woman with significant influence in the New Testament (Christian) church. She was the wife of Aquila. The couple were hospitable and devout. Their names are mentioned five times in the Bible, always together, which is indicative of a very close relationship. Two times, they are referred to as Aquila and Priscilla. Three times, they are referred to as Priscilla and Aquila. The latter might indicate the leadership influence that Priscilla had.

Priscilla and Aquila lived at a time when it was not popular to be Christian, but they were more than willing to make sacrifices for Christ and His church. They exhibited great Christian hospitality. The church members usually met in their home, wherever they lived. Driven from Italy by a decree of Emperor Claudius, the couple went by boat to Corinth. There, they met Paul the apostle, and soon afterward discovered they had much in common. Since all three were tent makers and persecuted Christians, they easily became friends. When Paul left Corinth, Priscilla and Aquila went with him.

Priscilla's life is worthy of emulating. She was not only a homemaker; she also assisted her husband in his business. She was versed in the Old Testament Scriptures. After she and her husband met Paul, she improved on the gifts that God had given her by applying herself to the study of the gospel of Jesus Christ. She learned the gospel in depth, which qualified her to teach it to others. Her new ability was proven to be a very useful one when she met the young Apollo. He was an eloquent man who was well versed in the Scriptures, although he knew only the teaching of John the Baptist, because he had been taught and baptized by John. Yet he spoke out boldly and irrefutably.

Quickly perceiving the limitations of Apollo's knowledge, Priscilla and Aquila invited him into their confidence and taught him the correct meaning, or interpretation, of the Scriptures. After this, the Scripture says, "He mightily convinced the Jews, and that publicly, showing by the scriptures that Jesus was the Christ."

Priscilla was a kind and supportive companion to her husband. She learned the family business. She was a devout Christian and Bible teacher. Hers is an exemplary life of consecration, self-sacrifice, and humility for the cause of Christ.

Today, there is no justification whatsoever for a Christian woman to be ignorant of the Scriptures. Information is readily available to men and women everywhere.

"Study to show thyself approved unto a God, a workman that needeth not to be ashamed, rightly dividing the word of truth" (2 Timothy 2:15).

# LOIS AND EUNICE

*Acts 16:1–3*
*2 Timothy 1:5; 3:14–15; 4:5*

Eunice, Lois, and Timothy lived together in Lystra, apparently in the same house.

## Lois

There are many grandmothers mentioned in the Bible, but only one is mentioned as having such an influential part in the training of her grandson. Lois was a devout Jewess who evidently instructed her daughter Eunice and her grandson Timothy in the ways of the Lord.

## Eunice

Eunice was the daughter of Lois and the mother of young Timothy. Eunice, a Jewess, married a Greek who was not a believer. His name is not mentioned in Scripture. Whether he was living or dead, we do not know. We do know that at the time when Paul met Timothy, Timothy had not been circumcised according to Jewish tradition, which was perhaps because of his Greek father's influence.

The outstanding thing about Lois and Eunice is their training of Timothy, their religious influence on Timothy, who, since the time of his childhood, knew the Scriptures. These mothers took

Proverbs 22:6 to heart. They trained him up in the way that he should go so that when he was old he did not depart from it.

Although this mother and grandmother were well versed in the Scriptures (of the Old Testament), it was Paul who taught them about and brought them to Christ.

The apostle Paul placed his approval upon Timothy when he said, "Let no man despise the gift that is within you" (1 Timothy 4:12). Paul took Timothy under his wing. Timothy became a young preacher eventually he became a bishop.

The lives of Eunice and Lois impress upon all that the most important work in a mother's life is the training of her children. These two women, Lois and Eunice are immortalized through their son Timothy – a child who knew the Holy Scriptures.

# PHOEBE

*Romans 16:1–2*

The name Phoebe indicates a sister, a servant, and/or a helper.

In just two short verses in the sixteenth chapter of Romans, Paul gives us a very approving look into the character of the devout Phoebe. She was a sister in the church, a servant of the church, and the helper of many, including Paul. The word *sister* is a term of endearment that indicates a spiritual relationship. The word *servant* is derived from *diakonos,* from which we get the word deaconess. A helper is one who appears and assists when there is a need. Phoebe was all of this and more.

Just how many were in the Roman church at the time, we are not told. But we do know that Phoebe is the only one mentioned by name, which signifies the high level of esteem in which she was held by Paul. He requested that the church in Rome render her respect as well.

The Scriptures do not tell us if Phoebe occupied some special position; it emphasizes her services rendered rather than her position held. Some have suggested that Phoebe was the first deaconess, or at least one of the first deaconesses, of the Christian church.

Various commentaries state that Cenchrea was a port in Corinth on the east side of the isthmus in the Saronic Gulf. It was here that Paul wrote the letter to the Roman Christians (the book of Romans). Presumably, Phoebe carried the epistle from Cenchrea to Rome, as private correspondence was sent by a friend or a messenger.

It appears that Phoebe was of notable economic status, as she planned a business trip to Rome and offered to take Paul's letter to the saints along with her.

There is a place for Phoebes in the church today, as the church needs women who prove themselves faithful in little things and who may also be entrusted to orchestrate grand and complex assignments.

May the Lord be able to say of all of us who professed the name, Christians, "Well done, good and faithful servant, you have been faithful over a few things, I will make you ruler over many things. Enter thou into the joy of your Lord" (Matthew 25:23).

# BERNICE AND DRUSILLA

*Acts 24:10–27; 25:13, 23; 26:30*

In Scripture, there is not much mentioned about the background of Bernice and Drusilla. But since they were public figures, we turn to public history records to find more information.

The Jewish historian Flavius Josephus tells us that they were sisters. Their father was Herod Agrippa I, which made them granddaughters of Herod the Great. Their father had three daughters: Bernice, the oldest; Mariamne, not mentioned in Scripture; and Drusilla, the youngest. It is said that Drusilla was more beautiful than her sisters, which caused much jealousy between them.

Bernice is mentioned three times in the book of Acts. She lived a very wicked and incestuous life. She was first married to Marcus. After his death, she became the wife of Herod of Chalcis, her own uncle. After his death, she had relations with Agrippa, her own brother, and with him listened to Paul's exhortation at Caesarea. Later, she was married to the king of Sicily. This marriage was of short duration, as she soon returned to Agrippa. She was later the mistress of Vespasian and Titus, who both finally cast her aside.

Drusilla married Aziaus, King of Emesa, at the age of fourteen. She soon left him for Felix, procurator of Judea, who had been captivated by her beauty and employed a Cyprian sorcerer to gain her for his wife. The couple had one son, Agrippa, who died in the eruption of Mount Vesuvius in Pompeii in AD 79. When Paul preached before Felix and Drusilla of righteousness, temperance, and judgment, Felix trembled but did not repent. How different their life story would have been if they had listened to and accepted Paul's message and repented.

"Today, if you will hear His voice, harden not your heart as in rebellion" (Psalm 95:7–8).

"Behold now is the accepted time; behold now is the day of salvation" (2 Corinthians 6:2).

# EUODIAS AND SYNTYCHE

*Philippians 4:2 Acts 16:13–15*

It seems that Paul preached to a group of women first in Philippi. Lydia was in that group, and, perhaps, so were Euodias and Syntyche.

When Paul exhorted these two church workers to be of the same mind in the Lord, he had perceived that there was a variance between them. What the subject of the matter was, we are not told. Undoubtedly, this dissention was hindering the well-being and progress of the church. We believe that Paul's counsel was not in vain, and this division was made right and the church moved on forward.

Are there any similar situations in your personal life or your church today? If so, then the same advice Paul gave to Euodias and Syntyche applies to you: " I Implore [name] and [name] to be of the same mind in the Lord" (Philippians 4:2).

# TRYPHENA AND TRYPHOSA

*Romans 16:12*

These two names are mentioned only one time in the Scriptures. Tryphena and Tryphosa are mentioned by name as women who toiled hard in doing the Lord's work. Paul mentioned them as he concluded the book of Romans. Elsewhere, the Scriptures are silent about Tryphena and Tryphosa. Judging by their names, we would perhaps think that Tryphena and Tryphosa were twins. We do not know. But we do know that they were certainly close kin. They must have been actively involved in serving the church at Rome— perhaps they were deaconesses, ushers, social directors, or prayer leaders. Otherwise, Paul would not have singled them out in his commendation of gratitude for their devoted labor in the Lord. In their own committed way, these active workers carved a niche for themselves in the Bible's gallery of saints.

In the book of Acts of the Apostles, we are told that during Paul's two years under house arrest in Rome, many in the household of Caesar were converted to Christianity. Tryphena and Tryphosa were probably among that number. It was the custom of that day for the emperors to provide a separate burial place for their servants. Tryphena and Tryphosa have both been identified in such a cemetery. Their graves are marked by a Christian inscription naming them among the saints of Caesar's house.

# Summary

The women whose lives we have studied are representative of all the women of the holy scriptures. This cross-section of named women of the Bible helps us to learn something of the cultural and religious background of the times which they lived and to see how they responded to their world in light of the roles assigned to them and how we, too, can respond to our world as we contrast these women's roles with our own today.

In the life sketches of the women we have studied we have caught glimpses of God's image as well as Satan's. Sometimes the choices they made, even among the most spiritual, identified more with Satan than with God.

Though our culture is obviously different and vastly remote from these women, we share many of the same emotional turmoils and struggles. We still agonize over infertility, worry about our children, long for real affection and struggle to find faith in times of uncertainty. By studying the women of the Bible, we can deepen our understanding of Scripture, experience more of God's love, recognize His profound jealousy and discover His omnipotent ability to bring good out of the most difficult and hopeless situations.

In summary, there are only two types of women, virtuous and non- virtuous. The lives of the virtuous women were Christ-centered. They centered their lives, their faith and all their perspective of the future on Christ and Christ alone. These are the Hannahs, the Deborahs, the Phoebes, the Lydias, etc. The non-virtuous or worldly women were all about themselves. Their lives were centered on "what can I get for myself"? Who do I have to miss-use to do that? It doesn't matter. Just as long as I come out on top. These are the Jezebels, the Atheliahs, the Deliliahs, the Bernices and Drusillas. You must identify with one or the other group. The undecided are looked upon by God the same as the non-virtuous and their end will be the same. Rev. 3:16.

Now the choice is yours. Which will you choose to emulate; virtuous or non-virtuous? I do hope you choose the former.

# Sources

Holy Bible, American King James Version.

Scripture quotations marked "NKJV" are taken from the New King James Version. Copyright © 1982 by Thomas Nelson, Inc. Used by permission. All rights reserved.

# R

Culwell, Kitty Jones. *Sarah's Daughters.* Murfreesboro: DeHoff Publications, 2006.

Deen, Edith. *All the Women of the Bible.* New York; Harper and Row, 1955.

Del Mastro, M. L. *All the Women of the Bible.* New York; Castle Books, 2006.

Lockyer, Herbert, RSL. *All the Women of the Bible. Grand Rapid;*

Zondervan Books.

MacArthur, John. *Twelve Extraordinary Women.* Dallas; Thomas Nelson, Inc., 2005.

*Matthew Henry's Commentary on the Whole Bible.* Peabody;Zondervan, 2008.

*Seventh-Day Adventist Bible Commentaries,* vols. 1–7. Washington, DC; Review and Herald Publishing Association, 1980.

Tenney, Merrill C. *The Zondervan Pictorial Bible Dictionary. Grand Rapids;* Zondervan Publishing House, 1967.

Whiston, A. M. *The Complete Works of Josephus. Nashville;.* Thomas Nelson, 1998.

White, Ellen G. *Acts of the Apostles. Nashville;* Pacific Press Publishing Assoc., 1917.

———. *The Desire of Ages. Nashville;* Pacific Press Publishing Assoc.,, 1917.

———. *Patriots and Prophets. Nashville;* Pacific Press Publishing Assoc., 1917.

———. *Prophets* and *Kings. Nashville;* Pacific Press Publishing Assoc., 1917.

# Judges of Israel

| # | Name | Tribe | Years Judged | Scripture |
|---|---|---|---|---|
| 1. | Othinel | Judah | 40 | Judges 3:9-11 |
| 2. | Ehud | Benjamin | 80 | Judges 3:15-30 |
| 3. | Shamgar | Judah | ? | Judges 3:31 |
| 4. | Deborah | Ephraim | 40 | Judges 4:4-5:31 |
|  | Barak | Naphtali |  |  |
| 5. | Gideon | Manasseh | 40 | Judges 6:7-8:35 |
| 6. | Abimelech | Manasseh | 3 | Judges 9:1-57 |
| 7. | Tala | Issachar | 23 | Judges 10:1-2 |
| 8. | Jair | Manasseh | 22 | Judges 10:3-5 |
| 9. | Jephthah | Manasseh | 6 | Judges 11:1-12:7 |
| 10. | Ibzan | Judah | 7 | Judges 12:8-10 |

| 11. | Elan | Zebulun | 10 | Judges 12:11-12 |
|-----|------|---------|----|-----------------|
| 12. | Abdon | Ephraim | 8 | Judges 12:1.3-15 |
| 13. | Samson | Dan | 20 | Judges 13:2-15:31 |
| 14 | Eli | Levi | 40 | |
| 15 | Samuel | Ephraim | 47 | Judges 21:25. |

# Kings of Israel and Judah

| Judah | | Israel | |
|---|---|---|---|
| King | Reigned | King | Reigned |
| Rehoboam | 17 | Jeroboam | 22 |
| Abijah | 3 | Nadab | 2 |
| Asa | 41 | Baasha | 24 |
| | | Elah | 2 |
| | | Zimri | 7 days |
| | | Omri | 12 |
| Johoshaphat | 25 | Ahab | 22 |
| Jehoram | 8 | Ahaziah | 2 |
| Ahaziah | 1 | Joram | 12 |
| Athaliah | 6 | Jehu | 28 |
| Joash | 40 | Jehoahaz | 1.7 |
| Amaziah | 29 | Jehoash | 16 |
| Uzziah | 52 | Jeroboam II | 41 |

| | | | |
|---|---|---|---|
| Jotham | 16 | Zechariah | 6 mos. |
| Ahaz | 16 | Shallum | 1 mos. |
| Hezekiah | 29 | Menahem | 10 |
| Manasseh | 55 | Pekahiah | 2 |
| Amon | 2 | Pekah | 20 |
| Josiah | 31 | Hoshea | 9 |
| Jehoahaz/ Shallum | 3 | 722 BC Fall of Samaria to Assyria | |
| Jehoiakim | 11 | | |
| Jehoiachin | 3 mos | | |
| Zdekiah | 11 | | |

Jehoahaz/Shallum - Taken prisoner to Egypt by Pharaoh - 609 BC.

Jehoiakim - Died in Jerusalem 598 Be.

Zedekiah - Taken prisoner to Babylon by Nebuchadnezzar 586 Be.

Jehoichin/Jeconiah -Taken prisoner to Babylon by Nebuchadnezzar with Ezekial.